The
Poet's
Work

AN INTRODUCTION TO CZESLAW MILOSZ

Leonard Nathan
and
Arthur Quinn

Harvard University Press
Cambridge, Massachusetts, and London, England
1991

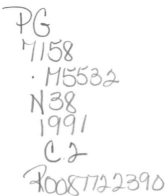

Copyright © 1991 by the President and
Fellows of Harvard College

All rights reserved

Printed in the United States of America

10 9 8 7 6 5 4 3 2 1

This book is printed on acid-free paper, and its binding materials
have been chosen for strength and durability.

Library of Congress cataloging information is on last page of book.

Contents

Foreword

As if literary history itself had overcome, by way of exception, its usual dislike for round figures, this book will appear in bookstores almost exactly eighty years after its subject was born (on June 30, 1911), sixty years after he cofounded, as a student at Stefan Batory University in Wilno, the pathbreaking poetry group Zagary, forty years after he asked for political asylum in France and became an emigré, thirty years after he settled permanently in the United States, and ten years after his triumphant return to Poland in the wake of the Nobel Prize in literature (awarded to him in 1980). Viewed from the less global perspective of Cambridge, Massachusetts, the publication of this book also marks the tenth anniversary of Czeslaw Milosz's Charles Eliot Norton Lectures at Harvard, published later as *The Witness of Poetry* by Harvard University Press.

Faced with this list of anniversaries, which add up to a miniaturized review of Milosz's career, and reminded once again of Joseph Brodsky's well-known description of Milosz as "one of the greatest poets of our time, perhaps the greatest," readers may experience genuine astonishment upon learning that the volume they have just opened is actually the first book-length introduction to the Polish poet's work written by American critics. The few books on Milosz available in English are either, like Aleksander Fiut's *The Eternal Moment: The Poetry of Czeslaw Milosz,* studies written originally in Polish by a Polish author or, all their merits notwithstanding, collections of essays written on selected works and topics without aspiring to a comprehensive picture or methodic presentation, as is the case of Donald Davie's otherwise penetrating *Czeslaw Milosz and the Insufficiency of Lyric.* In addition, numerous essays on Milosz and reviews of his books, ranging from brilliant to banal and from insightful to insipid, can be found in American literary periodicals and collections of essays of individual critics; still none of these works can serve as a detailed and fully reliable introduction even to the body of Milosz's writings available in English, not to mention the entirety of his oeuvre.

The emigré poet's reception in the language, culture, and society that together form his second, adopted homeland—that special issue of comparative literary history is still waiting for its explorer. The very formulation of the methodology of such an exploration would be a highly complex task, involving disciplines as diverse as cultural semiotics, the theory of translation, and the sociology of literature, to name but a few. To follow all these diverse lines at once would reveal many factors that have combined to delay the recognition of Milosz's poetic work in the west. One of these factors is, obviously enough, of a linguistic nature: the difficulty of translating poetry in general is even greater in the case of largely incompatible languages such as Polish and English. As if that were not enough, among twentieth-century Polish poets Milosz is one of the hardest to translate. On an imaginary scale of difficulty, his work, to be sure, would be placed below such language prestidigitators and experimenters as Boleslaw Lesmian or Miron Bialoszewski, but far above Wislawa Szymborska, Zbigniew Herbert, or in particular Tadeusz Rozewicz.

Another factor has to do with history, politics, and demands of the literary market. After he became an emigré, Milosz sacrificed a considerable part of his time and creative energy to capturing the attention of western audiences by writing essays and works of fiction (*The Captive Mind* and *The Seizure of Power* are two examples) addressed directly to them and dealing with the most burning political issues of the day, such as the fate of Central Europe under Communist rule and the ominous spread of what was later called the "totalitarian temptation" among western intellectuals. Thus his literary career and reception in the west suffered for many years from a sort of optical distortion: his fame as a political essayist grew disproportionately, while his achievement as a poet was recognized almost exclusively by his Polish readers. (Even that recognition, by the way, was far off the mark because of another set of extraliterary factors. During the first three decades of Milosz's exile, his poetry enjoyed only a limited popularity among Polish emigré readers, a cultural community for the most part too much bent on preserving traditional values to appreciate his innovative work; and in Poland itself, at least until the mid-seventies, readers were almost completely barred from his work by Communist censorship.)

It was not until Milosz took the promotion of his poetry in the west into his own hands and began to translate it into English himself (helped by numerous American collaborators, some of them his Berkeley graduate students) that it started making its way to international recognition. The publication of his *Selected Poems* in 1973 marks the beginning of what can be called his career as a poet in America, if not an American poet.

The American critics who took interest in his work, however, faced a complicated set of hindrances and difficulties, alleviated only recently by the publication of his *Collected Poems, 1931–1987* in 1988. Before this book's appearance, the American critic could feel justifiably uncertain in dealing with Milosz's poetry. If one was not able to read the Polish originals, one could never be sure, first, to what extent the part of Milosz's output made available to the English-speaking reader was representative of the entirety of the poet's work; second, to what extent the contents and the inner order of the four collections Milosz had published in English reflected the pattern of his evolution; and third, perhaps most important, to what extent the translation was able to render the original quality of the work. If we add the fact that during the 1960s and 1970s Milosz's essayistic work, of which not *The Captive Mind* but, rather, books such as *The Land of Ulro* were becoming increasingly representative, also remained largely unknown to the English-speaking audience and thus could not serve as an aid in critical interpretation, it is not surprising that no comprehensive book on Milosz was written until now by American critics.

Still it might be said that the critics let themselves be intimidated too much. After all, Milosz's English output is not just another example of the typical situation in which an exotic author's work is presented to a western audience in some accidentally selected fragments by an accidentally appointed translator who is not necessarily an expert on this particular author's work. On the contrary, Milosz's is a unique case of a poet who either translates himself into a foreign language or actively collaborates with his translators, the latter being veritable Milosz specialists. In other words, English versions of his books present us with a rare opportunity of dealing with translations that, even though they may differ to some extent from the original for natural linguistic and cultural reasons, are still texts for which Milosz assumes total responsibility.

Under such circumstances, what might seem self-contradictory—a critic's attempt to give Milosz's work a holistic interpretation while dealing only with that part of his work available in English—can be taken as a fully legitimate effort. At this point the translated part covers nearly all of the poet's oeuvre, while the translation itself, instead of being a veil dimming the radiance of the original meanings, offers the reader exactly the meanings that the author himself has taken care to preserve in the even brighter light of his second language. Further, the critic's attempt to introduce the English-speaking reader to Milosz's work viewed as a whole is more than simply legitimate if the critics in question are Leonard Nathan and Arthur Quinn, two of the poet's Berkeley colleagues. Their thorough familiarity with Milosz's poetry, fiction, and essays (in Nathan's case, the special familiarity of a cotranslator of many of the most difficult poems) is a result of not merely close reading of the texts but also of discussing them in long detail with the author. For Milosz's Polish readers, such as myself, there is nothing in Nathan and Quinn's book that would not be confirmed by what a reading of the poet's other, so far untranslated works might bring in; and there is, as well, a great deal to learn here. This book is no doubt just what Milosz's work needs as the poet reaches his eightieth year: a way of looking back at his six decades of writing to discover the underlying unity.

Stanislaw Baranczak

For in this period the poet's work is done: and all the great
Events of time start forth and are conceived in such a period—
Within a moment: a pulsation of the artery.

William Blake, Milton, plate 29

1
San
Francisco
Bay

Czeslaw Milosz's *Visions from San Francisco Bay,* a collection of essays
first published in Polish in 1969 almost a decade after he arrived at
Berkeley, has been the most neglected of his translated works. At first
glance the neglect is surprising, for this book could be for most
American readers the best introduction to Milosz's work as a whole.
Here in a series of short essays Milosz presents more plainly than
anywhere else his view of the human condition. But this is precisely
what explains the neglect: Milosz's vision of our predicament is
enough to make any complacent reader wince.

To be sure, *Visions from San Francisco Bay* was widely reviewed
when it came out in 1982. And all the reviews we read were positive,
respectful, sometimes enthusiastic, always full of good cheer. It was
the good cheer that bothered us. The reviewer in the *San Francisco
Chronicle* liked the book because here one could learn the poet's
response to highways, underground newspapers, sidewalk preachers,
supermarkets. Reading this review was like watching Milosz himself
being trimmed and put under cellophane for supermarket display,
somewhere between the capers and the fresh salmon. The best of the

reviews—and a careful, intelligent essay it was—bore the title "The Devil and Mr. Milosz." Here was that good cheer again, the demonic voices evoked by Milosz rechanneled to sound amusing, as if from George Bernard Shaw or *The Screwtape Letters*. Milosz was being praised into inconsequence.[1]

Visions from San Francisco Bay itself offers a description and explanation of this strange process, with respect not to Milosz himself but rather to the California poet Robinson Jeffers. Milosz believes that Jeffers was not taken seriously by his contemporaries because he tried to break through an "invisible web of censorship." "One must recall that he was neglected by people who placed great value on meat, alcohol, comfortable houses, and luxurious cars, and tolerated words as if they were harmless hobbies" (VSF, 93).

Make Milosz's work a mere exercise in autobiographical expression; make it an intriguing commentary on the vagaries of twentieth-century history; make it a convenient opportunity to express ringing support for Solidarity or to praise the remarkable range in modern poetry. But when Milosz says that the demonic is at the core of contemporary life, when he says that the highest function of discourse is exorcism or that poets should pray that "good spirits, not evil ones, choose us for their instruments"—surely he must be speaking figuratively. It would be indecorous to take him at his word. Such a way of talking must be for a man so sophisticated, sensitive, accomplished, only a harmless hobby.

Visions of San Francisco Bay could have been the title of one of those lovely coffeetable books produced by the Sierra Club perhaps, filled with Ansel Adams photographs of the earthly paradise. Milosz does find much to praise in the western American landscape. Yet, even as he praises it, he confesses that there is "something oppressive in the virginity of this country" (8). He values the splendid landscapes for making him experience oppression.

One of the poets with whom Milosz was associated in Poland during World War II, Mieczyslaw Jastrun, wrote in 1944: "And far more hostile, more indifferent / Than all that common and inhuman grave / Is the beauty of the earth" (HPL, 461). The hostile beauty of the earth is central to *Visions of San Francisco Bay*. In Death Valley, in the Sierras, in a redwood forest where eagles circle above chasms of mist, Milosz sees an alien, inhuman place, something neither good nor bad, however tempted we might be to find comfort in its physical beauty. Such a place can be used as a "screen where people's inner hells and heavens are projected"—but in itself it is only a "chaos which dispenses with valuation" (VSF, 10).

The European landscape can easily be imagined as humane, as but a stage for human strivings, shaped by human values. The American West does not permit such comforting delusions. "Both here, on the West Coast, and everywhere in America, one is faced with something that is impossible to define by allusions to the 'humanistically formed imagination,' something incomprehensible in regard both to the forms taken in by the eye and to the connection those forms have to the lives of human beings" (8). If we wince at this, Milosz assures us that he winces too. Yet he insists that in this discomfort we are coming close to the heart of the European immigrant experience, which is so often romanticized. "People decided to leave their villages in the same spirit as a man considers suicide; they weighed everything, then went off into the unknown, but once there, they were seized by a despair unlike anything they had ever experienced in the old country" (42). They had, if unwillingly, broken through the cocoon of constantly renewed interdependencies that shielded them from the real world. In America they could for the first time see it for what it was, in and of itself, an alien and indifferent thing. They could taste "the elixir of pure alienation" and in their loneliness perceive the human condition.

Or this at least seems to have been Milosz's own experience: "Now I seek shelter in these pages, but my humanistic zeal has been weakened by the mountains and the ocean, by those many moments when I have gazed upon boundless immensities with a feeling akin to nausea, the wind ravaging my little homestead of hopes and intentions" (11). But Milosz himself, like any human being, and unlike the impersonal force called nature, cannot and will not dispense with valuation. An indifferent universe is to him an evil universe. He finds precedent for this dark conclusion in the old Manichean heresy which taught that the little good in this world was trapped here as if in exile, yearning for escape. This conclusion Milosz finds empirically confirmed not just in the horrors of modern history but in the teaching of modern evolutionary biology:

> Obviously, the struggle with Evil in the Universe is an old one; the Manicheans were among the first who refused to believe such a miserable world could issue from the hands of a God who was good . . . Yet, never was the position of those who defend the idea of a hidden harmony more difficult, never was Manichean ferocity more aggressive than when the nineteenth century observed that the suffering of living matter is the mainspring of its Movement and that the individual creature is sacrificed in the name of a splendid and enormous transformation without goal or purpose. (23–24)

Some species rise, others fall, as do human families, nations, and whole civilizations. There may well be an internal logic to these transformations, a logic that when viewed from sufficient distance has its own elegance, harmony, and grace. Our reason tempts us to be enthralled by this superhuman splendor; but when so enthralled we find it difficult to remember, except perhaps as an element in an abstract calculus, the millions of individuals, the millions upon millions, who unwillingly paid for this splendor with pain and blood.

The call of nature—survival of the fittest—and the call of history—the strong do what they will, the weak what they must—are a single song, a siren song that would have us lose our sense of "dread and repugnance for the impersonal cruelty built into the structure of the universe." This song governs our world: "The fear of hell-fire has not vanished; hell . . . has taken root in our very subjugation to and helplessness against the natural forces residing in us, which today are the domain of the biologist, doctor, scientist, psychiatrist" (24). Hell is the subjection of the human to the inhuman, of the personal to the impersonal, of the living to the dead, of the concrete to the abstract. In hell the elemental wonder at mere existence is lost; everything becomes a case, an instance, a symptom. So we must not mistake systematic philosophy or science for allies in our struggle against the inhuman, for they by their very nature attempt to reduce the world to abstractions.

For Milosz philosophical systems are worth studying only in order to dismiss them. And science? "Had I a liking for the sciences, perhaps only a sociology which examines the self-confident social sciences would satisfy me. Fortunately, I do not, for I would then have used the garb of a scientific shaman to conceal my own preferences and biases" (63).

But what of the great achievements of technology, which at least in its benign applications has alleviated human suffering and otherwise made human beings less dependent on the vicissitudes of nature? About even these achievements Milosz has deep doubts. He suggests that this could well be the subtlest deception of the demonic. "The greatest trick of this continent's demons, their leisurely vengeance, consists in surrendering nature, recognizing that it could not be defended; but in place of nature there arose that civilization which to its members appears to be Nature itself, endowed with nearly all the features of that other nature" (68).

The superhuman landscape has been conquered only by a superhuman technology—but this conquest proves pyrrhic. The technology itself now dwarfs the individual into inconsequence, and far more effectively because now we are being dwarfed by the products of our own collectivity. We feel reduced to "impotence, evasion, a solitude with phonograph music and a fire in the fireplace" (68). Unless, that is, we are willing to assert what seems absurd, both to others and to ourselves: what we must assert is the primacy of the concrete, the personal, however ephemeral or inconsequential that may seem to our mind's eye. A landscape viewed from an airplane may well look like an image on a television screen. From such heights our perceptions suffer from ontological anemia. But even viewing such a washed-out scene, we can vivify it, though it becomes horrifying: "This continent is desolate, the skin of an antediluvian beast, flaxen, bluish, yellow, sometimes furry with forests" (67).

Milosz prefers to see the continent this way, as a real thing—and he claims to offer his preferences as merely personal. He does not aim to prove them true because proof always involves abstractions, and the devil always wins at his own game. But Milosz can continue to assert unyieldingly his preferences against the devil and his syllogisms, even at the risk of embarrassing his reader and himself in his persistent use of the outmoded language of demonology. If the world sacrifices the individual with apparent indifference, if reality seems governed by abstract laws, who is responsible for such a travesty? There must be agents behind all this, certain living creatures who are devoted to deluding us—and these agents have traditionally been denominated as evil spirits.

Milosz, when it involves him in what seems patent defiance of common sense, always strives to speak the language of the concrete, the personal. It is the language of poetry and essay: "The only thing we can do is try to communicate with one another" (5). Communicating our concrete presence, our uniqueness, will help us to resist the seductive voices of the demonic: "Whenever I take up my pen, which itself pretends to knowledge, since language is composed of affirmations and negations, I treat that act only as the exorcism of the evil spirits of the present" (226). Language will, left to itself, pretend to knowledge and reduce the concrete to propositions. Hence it must be handled with a certain recognition of danger. Language is a contradiction, at once sound and idea, just human beings are at once person and organism. And so Milosz begins his poem "Ars Poetica?": "I have always aspired to a more spacious form / that would be free from the claims of poetry or prose / and would let us understand each other without exposing / the author or reader to sublime agonies" (BW, 30). Such a communication of individuality or uniqueness is not possible except through the mediation of a language full of claims. The communication can be achieved only by turning this language against itself, by irony, by self-contradiction, and by the sublime agony of attempting to transcend the very language. There is no art of poetry except one that ends in a question mark.

Much of culture, much of the invisible web of censorship, is meant to "mask man's fundamental duality" (VSF, 53): to mask the duality and thereby free people from the necessity of choice. Milosz's work is devoted to unmasking that duality; he wants to make his readers admit the contradictory nature of their own experience. Milosz agrees with Simone Weil that contradiction is the lever of transcendence. Contradiction forces us to assert our preferences as preferences, to make an "arbitrary choice, not subject to verification." We must recognize that we are living within the contradiction; it is not a "background against which to play out our tragicomedies" (29). Our personalism, our humanism, if such we choose, will scarcely be comforting. It will be a "piety without a home," which "fortunately, allows me no safe superiority" (34). (Superiority would come only if we knew we were right.) Perhaps this half-ironic piety is best summarized in the title of one essay: "An Essay in Which the Author Confesses That He Is on the Side of Man, for Lack of Anything Better."

Actually he also confesses that he is on the side of God, who presumably is somewhat better. But Milosz's is not the God of philosophers or theologians. "I desire a God . . . who would love me and help me in misfortune, who would save me from the nothingness of death, to whom I could each day render homage and gratitude. God should have a beard and stroll the heavenly pastures" (77). Only a thoroughly anthropomorphic religion can resist "the exact sciences which annihilate the individual" (82).

Even the summary of *Visions* we have just presented does in one important respect violate the spirit of the book. To say that the choice for Milosz is a choice between the abstract and the concrete, between logic and contradiction, is to state the choice wrongly, because it is an abstraction. The choice for Milosz is never between ideas, world views, or philosophies; it is always between persons. At the cosmic level Milosz may think the choice is between a bearded God and sophisticated demons. But in the small world of *Visions from San Francisco Bay* it is a choice between Milosz himself and the great, neglected Robinson Jeffers.

Jeffers in his way was as unyielding as Milosz. He saw essentially the same contradictions as Milosz, the same dualities at the heart of human experience—and saw too the absolute necessity of choice. Jeffers just chose contrarily, to celebrate the impersonal. His god was pure motion, and he seemed to consider consciousness itself an unforgivable flaw. We might think that between such opposite valuations no communication would be possible. Perhaps this would be so, if logic did really rule, if communication took place between valuations or positions and not between persons.

But Jeffers wrote in the language of poetry, a language that forces dialogue. And so Milosz, as he wandered Monterey and wondered at this fellow poet's life, found himself forced into dialogue. The result was "To Robinson Jeffers," the only poem in *Visions from San Francisco Bay* and its centerpiece. Milosz addresses the alien poet, the dead but somehow still present Jeffers: "If you have not read the Slavic poets, / so much the better. There is nothing there / for a Scotch-Irish wanderer to seek." And he describes the forbidding world Jeffers praises: "Prayers are not heard. Basalt and granite. / Above them a bird of prey. The only beauty." Having conjured up such an overwhelming presence, he has doubts: "What have I to do with you?" Even despair: "Oh, consolations of mortals, creeds futile!" But finally he finds within himself the power, albeit qualified and momentary, to contradict:

> And yet you did not know what I know. The earth teaches
> more than does the nakedness of elements. No one with
>   impunity
> gives himself the eyes of a god . . .
> Better to carve suns and moons on the joints of crosses
> as was done in my district. To birches and firs
> give feminine names. To implore protection
> against the mute and treacherous might
> than to proclaim, as you did, an inhuman thing.

2
Poland

A reader of *Visions from San Francisco Bay* who wishes to understand Milosz better might think to turn to his comprehensive study—written in English—of the Polish literary tradition, *The History of Polish Literature*, published in 1969. Consciously modeled on Gustave Lanson's *Historie de littérature française,* Milosz's study offered a brief interpretation of every significant Polish writer—including the prominent twentieth-century poet, novelist, and essayist, Czeslaw Milosz. For Milosz, who so often prided himself on being an esoteric writer accessible to a mere handful of readers, the prospect of summarizing his own work in a few sentences was a task at once embarrassing and distasteful. Nonetheless he complied with the requirements of the survey, although referring to himself in the third person: "Critics have tended to see a myth of the Earth, a protective deity ever renewing herself, as the core of Milosz's poetry . . . It is not certain whether this is true, since Christian elements are also strong" (HPL, 413).

To anyone who has just read *Visions* Milosz's insistence on the Christian elements in his work is not surprising; these elements dominate it. What will be surprising is that Milosz admits the just-ness of the pantheistic interpretation of these early poems; he says that the Christian elements are *also* strong, which implies that the pantheistic interpretation must be at least partly correct. From *Visions* we might think that the fundamental choice is between pantheism and Christianity, and that Milosz is clearly on the side of Christianity. But his treatment of his own work in *History* suggests that things are not quite so simple. Pantheism and Christianity have now been presented as a dialectical tension *within* Milosz's own work. All that we can conclude from *Visions* is that Robinson Jeffers' kind of pan-theism is unacceptable to the *mature* Milosz. Perhaps he has found a formulation of pantheism that does not seem incompatible with his Christianity, and perhaps a younger Milosz would have found Jeffers acceptable. The first step toward understanding how Milosz could be characterized as a "pure pantheist" (and why he himself will object only mildly to this epithet) is to find some examples of his writing that do seem pantheistic. Such examples are not hard to find, and they all have something else in common as well; they are poems from Milosz's earliest period, the 1930s, and were written in Wilno, Lithu-ania.

Milosz was then a founding member of a small group called Zagary, the Lithuanian word for *brushwood*, which, in Milosz's own gloss, had developed a far more specific meaning in his locale: the word meant "dry twigs half charred in fire but still glowing" (HPL, 412). A whole poetics was implicit in this image. Human beings are so much brushwood in the cosmic scheme of things; we come to be and pass away in a moment. Yet in the conflagrations that reduce us to charred cinders, as we pass into nothingness, we can still struggle to give off some light, which is our only way to affirm the value of the very process that consumes us. This glowing ember of human suffering is called poetry. As Milosz later put it, "Man perishes entire and leaves no trace except a spark of beauty, provided he can trap it" (LU, 20).

Many of Milosz's poems of the Zagary period are tributes to pantheism, celebrations of the renewal of earth. In "Hymn" (1935) he

praises the earth that would soon dispense with him as if he had never
existed:

> Roll on, rivers; raise your hands,
> cities! I, a faithful son of the black earth, shall return to the
>   black earth,
> as if my life had not been.   (SP, 35)

Despite the recognition of his own transience, Milosz is a faithful son
of earth. Only then will he—and we through him—be able to address nature directly: "There is no one between you and me / and to
me strength is given." Only then will her children be able to draw
strength from mother earth, and only then will the poet be able to
view human transience with equanimity:

> Seasons come and go, men and women mate,
> children in half-sleep run their hands across the wall
> and draw lands with a finger wet with saliva.
> Forms come and go, what seemed invincible, crumbles.   (36)

To nature he can say that all human effort exists only here

> so that you may crush it, so that you step on it,
> so that your breath move the wheel
> and a frail structure shake with motion,
> so that you give to it hunger and to others wine, salt and bread.
>   (36–37)

Milosz has said of "Hymn" that it is the most pantheistic of all his
poems. The poet is one who can find words for intimate contact with
the world, who can express the essential goodness of the whole.
Nature chooses those, the poets, who are fully open to its inspiration
and its dictation. So Milosz remembers that "Hymn" was "almost
'*ecriture automatique*,'" composed in "one go" as if he were being
given words he did not entirely understand. Like the poem itself, his
experience in writing it was a "merging with change and movement."
The ultimate instance of this experience would be "the ecstasy of
death." It is for this reason that Milosz associated the poem with his

attraction to the work of the poet Jaroslaw Iwaszkiewicz (1894–
1980)—"because of its constant erotic and thanatological sweetness"
(CCM, 108–110).[1]

Milosz of course realized that pantheism in praise of sweet death
would not be palatable to many. In 1934 he had written "The Song"
(SN 90–95), a lyric dialogue between a chorus and a woman fright-
ened by her own mortality. The woman prays to the earth:

> I am afraid to stay alone here, I have nothing but my body
>   . . . Earth
> do not abandon me.

The chorus responds to this would-be unfaithful daughter of the
black earth by cataloguing the joys of physical existence, concluding:

> All joy comes from the earth, there is no delight without her,
> Man is given to the earth only, let him desire no other.

But the woman wants more than the transience that the earth grants
her, and she begins to pray to God to set her free "from earth's
caresses." The chorus now firmly assures her that praying is self-
delusion; she must accept the fact that

> Everything comes from the earth, she is perfect . . .
> Everything comes from the earth and returns to her.

Still the woman wants more, permanence, immortality, but in the
end she can neither believe in her own hopes nor accept the chorus'
consolation:

> But there is nothing in me but fear,
> nothing but the running of dark waves.
> I am the wind that blows in dark waters, disappearing,
> I am the wind going out and not coming back,
> milkweed pollen on the black meadows of the world.

In the very expression of her fear she has in effect admitted the
superiority of the earth because, through language, she has made that
fear part of the natural economy. She sees herself as pollen on the

black meadows of the world. And then suddenly, without explanation, both she and the chorus disappear like pollen, to leave only some unspecified "last voices" to conclude the poem. Their conclusion is hardly a conclusion at all, for it is not logically connected with what has gone before. It is simply praise of existence, praise that does not notice the disappearance of the woman and her chorus of consolers. Milosz will not give his chorus the last word because he does not want us to think that the splendors of nature are there as a consolation for human beings. They are just there, beautifully indifferent to human conversations about them.

In "Slow River" Milosz uses contrasting voices to show how difficult it is for human beings to accept natural beauty as an end in itself. He begins with the speaker of the poems expressing such an acceptance:

> There has not been for a long time
> a spring as beautiful as this one . . .
> In such a season, every voice becomes for us
> a shout of triumph. Glory, pain and glory
> to the grass, to the clouds, to the green oak wood.
> The gates of the earth torn open, the key to the earth revealed.

This paean is suddenly interrupted by the presence of another, to whom the speaker says:

> Why does this heat
> and depth of hatred radiate
> from your narrowed eyes? To you the rule,
> for you clouds in golden rings
> play a music, maples by the road exalt you.
> The invisible rein on every living thing
> leads to your hand.

The worship of nature at the beginning of the poem is contrasted with the human-centered conviction of the "you." Everything in nature is there for human use. A choric voice explains this attitude: "My brothers, avid for pleasure, smiling, beery, / have the world for a granary, a house of joy." Another voice, however, comes in to contradict. This human-centered view paradoxically impoverishes human existence itself, reduces humanity to a "dark rabble" and nature to "heaps of foods and mosses stomped ash-gray." The human-centered perception of nature, a drive to dominate rooted in hatred, is self-destructive. So the speaker of the poem attempts to resolve the conflict by an incantation that will absorb even the drive to dominate into the processes of nature:

> Three times must the wheel of blindness
> turn, before I look without fear at the power
> sleeping in my own hand, and recognize spring,
> the sky, the seas, and the dark, massed land.
> Three times will the liars have conquered
> before the great truth appears alive
> and in the splendor of one moment
> stand spring and the sky, the seas, the lands.

Clearly the slow river of nature is superior to any human effort to divert or deny it. If it were not, it would not be the divine earth.[2]

In "To Father Ch." Milosz evokes a renewal of the earth that will seem catastrophic from a human perspective:

> a stream of boiling lava
> will extinguish the cities and Noah will not escape in his ark.

Even to this we should be reconciled—indeed, we must regard it as somehow sacramental:

> We are reconciled after long antagonism,
> knowing that not a stone will remain standing
> of human happiness,
> The earth will stretch wide its jaws and in its echoing cathedral
> the last pagans will be baptized.[3]

Looking back at his poetry of this period, Milosz almost seems shocked by it. His celebration of what were, from the human perspective, catastrophes he could only attribute to immaturity: "Who knows if it was not precisely this impossibility of bringing order to my personal problems that caused me to nourish myself so passionately for several years on catastrophic visions, borrowing from the Marxists little more than their belief in a spasm of history? The impending annihilation was sweet: it would resolve everything; individual destiny lost its significance, all would become equal" (NR, 173).

These early poems are full of the terrible, things as "terrible as the earth's happiness," he writes in "Dawns." There he protests:

> Not enough one life is not enough.
> I'd like to live twice on this sad planet . . .
> And probe the laws to which the time was subject,
> Time that howled above us like a wind.   (CP, 16–17)

Stanislaw Baranczak has called "Dawns" a "poem on human fate, both collective and individual, subordinated by both historical processes and the processes of aging and death."[4] That summary could serve for many of the poems of this period. In "The Gates of the Arsenal" (CP, 10–12) even what is taken to be the highest human good works to our destruction; eyebrows are "Ripped apart by wisdom" and illumination kills; "touched by light, all that lives dies." In "Statue of a Couple" (CP, 21–22) the poet evokes the tombstone of lovers and finds all that can be said of them embodied in their unanswered cry: "What was it, what is it, what will it be."

Faced with the poignancy of such cries, Milosz often finds himself unable to affirm the goodness of the processes that destroy human individuality, or of time that howls above us like the wind. Even in poems that celebrate the earth and all its terrible beauties, he can never quite silence the distressed voice of the woman from "The Song." For instance, in the 1936 poem "Encounter" Milosz seems to celebrate even more the wonder that comes from recognizing the transience of things. Hares, humans, sensations, all are ephemeral:

We were riding through frozen fields in a wagon at dawn.
A red wing rose in the darkness.

And suddenly a hare ran across the road.
One of us pointed to it with his hand.

That was long ago. Today neither of them is alive,
Not the hare, nor the man who made the gesture.

O my love, where are they, where are they going
The flash of a hand, streak of movement, rustle of pebbles.
I ask not out of sorrow, but in wonder.   (BW, 3)

"Encounter," however, also suggests in its muted tones the inadequacy of mere meditation as a response to the transience of things. Although the last stanza ends with the speaker claiming that he is without emotion, it begins with strong feeling, so strong that the speaker stumbles and has to repeat himself: "O my love, where are they, where are they going." The poem is full of the very regret that the speaker tries to deny.

In other poems this regret is not just personal but also social. In "A Book in the Ruins" (CP, 28–30), he first describes "the hostile, marvelous times" in which his generation was destined to live. "It was an epoch of storm, the day of apocalypse, / old nations were destroyed, capitals turning / like a spindle, drunk under the foaming sky." And then he denies his readers the consolation that they might be rewarded for their suffering:

The laurel is not for us, aware of the punishment
which time allots to those who loved
temporality, deafened by the din of metals.
Thus we were marked to create a fame—nameless,
like a farewell shout of those departing—into darkness.

Despite poems like "Hymn" and "A Book," we are left wondering when Milosz concluded that pure pantheism was inadequate and what exactly led him to that conclusion. Again, we do not have to look far for the answer.

*   *   *

The Nazi occupation of Warsaw may not have been the end of all things human, but many thousands were falling, nameless, into the darkness each week. Belief was hard to sustain in the doomed city, beauty hard to find in its burning embers.

> Bees build around red liver,
> Ants build around black bone.
> It has begun: the tearing, the trampling on silks,
> It has begun: the breaking of glass, wood, copper, nickel, silver,
>   foam
> Of gypsum, iron sheets, violin strings, trumpets, leaves, balls,
>   crystals.
> Poof! Phosphorescent fire from yellow walls
> Engulfs animal and human hair.   (CP, 64)

So begins "A Poor Christian Looks at the Ghetto," with a catastrophic catalogue unlike those of Milosz's prewar poetry; no beauty here, only ruthless indifference. This is the Warsaw ghetto after its destruction, where the indifference—"Bees build around a red trace. / Ants build around the place left by my body"—is not ours, but the indifference of nature, an indifference that only increases our disgust. And the deity of this earth is not some benign personification of natural processes:

> Slowly, boring a tunnel, a guardian mole makes his way,
> With a small red lamp fastened to his forehead.
> He touches buried bodies, counts them, pushes on,
> He distinguishes human ashes by their luminous vapor,
> The ashes of each man by a different part of the spectrum.

The speaker cannot look on him with dispassion: "I am afraid, so afraid of the guardian mole." He is afraid because he knows he will be called to account: "What will I tell him . . . ? / My broken body will deliver me to his sight / And he will count me among the helpers of death: / The uncircumcised."

The interpretative temptation this poem leaves us with is to determine the identity of the strange "guardian mole." Milosz, however, has warned us away from any such attempt. When asked, he responded emphatically, "I don't know who the guardian mole is. The poem is simply an image of an earth full of ashes" (CCM, 132)—of an earth full of ashes and a speaker full of guilt. The guilt is not from some specific moral failing or responsibility for the catastrophe of the Warsaw ghetto; but neither need it be something so broad as "survivors' guilt," the collective guilt of Christians.[5] This poet, after all, had already been calling forth cataclysms, imagining that he might sing of their sweetness. It is hard not to see the bitter conclusion of "Days of Generation," for instance, as referring to the poet himself:

> It is your destiny so to move your wand,
> To wake up storms, to run through the heart of storms,
> To lay bare a monument like a nest in a thicket,
> Though all you wanted was to pluck a few roses.   (CP, 32)

Milosz and the other "catastrophists" waved their wands, and monumental storms were awakened.

They may have thought they could pluck a few roses in the midst of catastrophe. Now in Warsaw he and his associates were being called to account by the guardian mole (bestial projection of a subterranean guilt?). They had to admit that catastrophes were pure evil. How could they preserve their belief in the inherent goodness of nature? They would have to contend that, as Milosz puts it in the description of his Warsaw period in *History of Polish Literature,* "relapses into chaos, though ever-recurring, are not ultimate" (458–459).

Milosz was heartened in his efforts at affirmation by his discovery of William Blake.

> I acquired my English in wartime Warsaw—self-taught, but enough to read the poets. In one anthology, I came across a few of Blake's poems . . . In those times and in that landscape so inhospitable to a child's awe before the miraculous, Blake restored me to my earlier raptures, perhaps to my true vocation, that of lover. My conversion to Blake was, at that time, an emotional one, for my understanding failed me the moment I began to ponder the meaning of individual poems and lines. (LU, 31)

Although he could not intellectually defend or even explain his conversion, he sought to imitate Blake by finding goodness in the smallest and simplest of things. The same year he wrote "A Poor Christian" he also wrote a cycle of poems to celebrate the aspect of natural existence that he still worshipped. The cycle, titled significantly enough "The World" (CP, 36–55), is written like a child's primer—and Milosz himself calls it "one of the most serene in modern Polish literature" (HPL, 459). The tone, syntax, and diction are close to that of the fairy tale or nursery rhyme:

> On a seed of poppy is a tiny house,
> Inside it are people, a cat and a mouse.
> Outside in the yard, a dog barks at the moon.
> Then, in his one world, he sleeps until noon.[6]

To preserve oneself from utter despair, one must be able to return to the most innocent simplicity, to find the world in a poppy seed or a grain of sand.

The apparent simplicity of these poems, Milosz himself admits, is "somewhat deceptive . . . they are really a metaphysical tract, an equivalent, in colors and shapes, of the school blackboard . . . where Father Lallemant drew his Thomistic circles" (NR, 248). Milosz's allusion to Thomism—the Catholic theology based on the scholasticism of Thomas Aquinas—is a deeply considered one. He might not have been able to understand Blake on his own romantic terms; he could, however, assimilate Blake to his own traditional Catholic education (a training he continued in Warsaw). In the twenty poems that comprise "The World" Milosz tries to turn the reader back to this traditional wisdom, in part by ignoring the historical reality around writer and audience, and in this way starting with a blank slate, like a teacher beginning a class. For, as Donald Davie aptly notes, the cycle is "an idyll of education."[7]

The cycle follows children coming home from school, to the true source of their education, the family. Poem by poem we see them pass through various rooms and out into the world again, stages toward wisdom. It is not all light and love, this passage. After Mother, a supreme source of comfort, feeds them soup from a hot tureen (fourth poem), they must face on the narrow stairway a hideous boar's head, bestial fury in their own house. Shadows bring this trophy to life and Mother, as her shadow intersects that of the head, "struggles, alone, with the cruel beast" (fifth poem). Now their education begins in earnest; picture books that show the fate of man in images from the *Iliad* are brought up to date when a moth crushed by a child's hand "dies on the hero's body" (sixth poem). Then in Father's study the magic of reading is invoked (seventh poem). In the next group, his "serene wisdom" opens up the European world, its great cities, until they are ready to understand the "parable of the poppy seed" (eleventh poem):

> The Earth is a seed—and really no more,
> While other seeds are planets and stars.   (CP, 46)

So the very house in which they learn sits on a poppy seed, and in Mother's garden, in the peony bed, "one short instant equals a whole year" (twelfth poem). With their imaginations expanded in both space and time, the children can now confront the great spiritual verities—faith, hope, and charity. Faith is believing that all the world, evil itself, has a purpose. Rocks are here to hurt feet, a fact that is part of our necessary knowledge of things. "Hope is with you when you believe . . . / That all things you have ever seen here / Are like a garden looked at from a gate." Though we cannot enter to know it (is it paradise?) first hand, we are certain that it is there, just ahead. Charity is the desire to serve all things, without understanding why or how: "Who serves best doesn't always understand."

The children are now ready to confront the world, to leave the house for an outing in the woods, but this entails confronting death, those who have died and fled this world like birds:

> What is the earth for them? A lake of darkness.
> It has been swallowed by the night forever.
> They, above the dark as above black waves,
> Have their homes and islands, saved by the light.

Those left behind in the dark are afraid:

> The hot breath of the terrible beast
> Comes nearer and nearer, it belches its stench.

What the boar's head only suggests, bestial fury, pursues them now, not in the house but in a menacing outer darkness where they are exposed to every peril. Only Father can save them and they cry out:

> Where have you gone, Father? Why do you not pity
> Your children lost in this murky wood?

Father's answer is the reassurance that the darkness will pass, "the day will soon arise" and, with it, the bright world once more.

Now the children, and we, are ready for the final wisdom, "The Sun." In this concluding poem of the cycle, Milosz seems to side with the artist who wants to celebrate nature as a whole (as Milosz himself had earlier tried):

> All colors are from the sun. And it does not have
> any particular color, for it contains them all.
> And the whole Earth is like a poem
> While the sun above represents the artist.

But once we realize that Milosz expects us to recognize that the Sun represents God, the poem becomes a meditation on the relation between the Creator and his creatures, between the unity of being and the plurality of becoming. The great moral of this meditation is that we, as creatures, must not attempt to see with the eyes of God. A godlike vision of the whole is beyond our capacity:

> Whoever wants to paint the variegated world
> let him never look straight up at the sun
> Or he will lose the memory of things he has seen.
> Only burning tears will stay in his eyes.

The only way we can apprehend the whole and come to God is through small particulars:

Let him kneel down, lower his face to the grass,
And look at light reflected by the ground.
There he will find everything we have lost:
The stars and the roses, the dusks and the dawns.

Milosz can continue to worship the black earth, but only because it reflects a transcendent being. He has begun to find Christianity within his pantheism. But this kind of dilution raises its own problems, not the least of which is a deliberate and necessary ignorance of the overwhelming evil all around him, against which the father's assurance "Why this senseless fear?" must seem naive.

Whatever the limitations of pure pantheism, at least it provides a clear response to the problem of evil. What appears to us as evil is not really evil; we are simply observing from too narrow a perspective. The renewal of the great earth as a whole is the fundamental good to which all else, including our personal suffering, is secondary. Such a response is no longer available to Milosz, now that he has introduced a transcendent ground for the goodness of the earth.

He can maintain that creatures reflect their creator and that becoming contains being within it. Yet he has to explain why some creatures seem infernally separate from their creator, why some becoming seems to be intent on devouring being. Bullets are as real as clods of dirt or poppy seeds. Poppies can grow in the Warsaw ghetto. Milosz's world now comprises two contrary parts, which somehow coexist. How can the poppy exist in the same world as the guardian mole? Milosz has become a dualist, and this dualism is at the heart of "Song on the End of the World." It is a song of experience in marked contrast to the song of innocence that was "The World":

On the day the world ends
A bee circles a clover,
A fisherman mends a glimmering net.
Happy porpoises jump in the sea,
By the rainspout young sparrows are playing
And the snake is gold-skinned as it should always be. (SP, 57)

The world is ending, and prophets say that such apocalyptic cataclysms do reveal the ultimate meaning of things. Still Milosz envi-
sions the end of the world as simply the continuance of ordinary
things until the last moment. What of all the cataclysms, the extraordinary events? They have no place:

> And those who expected lightning and thunder
> Are disappointed.
> And those who expected signs and archangels' trumps
> Do not believe it is happening now.

What role is there for the prophet in this apocalypse of the ordinary?

> Only a white-haired old man, who would be a prophet
> Yet is not a prophet, for he's much too busy,
> Repeats while he binds his tomatoes:
> There will be no other end of the world,
> There will be no other end of the world.

Of course there seem to be extraordinary, even unique, events—
history at times does seem to have climaxes and purposes. But we
must realize that this is a delusion: Armageddon is a permanent
condition. We must seek the good in the ordinary things of this
world, not in its Armageddons. The Armageddons are only relapses
into chaos—and, though these are ever-recurring, we must believe
that they are not ultimate. To express this belief, to strengthen it, we
must give ourselves to the ordinary. Milosz once summarized the
most difficult wisdom he had learned from his experiences in Warsaw
during the Nazi terror by quoting Martin Luther. Luther, asked
what he would do if he knew the world was going to end tomorrow,
replied, "I would plant apple trees" (NR, 235).

So we should attend to the small tasks at hand, binding tomato
plants or planting an apple tree. But then, contrarily, should we avoid
the cosmic, prophetic tasks, such as singing a song on the end of the
world? Milosz's song is irony at the expense of high art. He is
proclaiming the inadequacy of songs that aspire to be more than

simple songs. Yet are the irony of a "Song for the End of the World" and the childlike simplicity of "The World," taken together, a sufficient response to the savagery he surrounding him? Milosz himself has insisted that "The World," when set against the Warsaw of 1943, was its exact opposite; hence, placed in historical context, it must be seen as "a rather ironic operation." It is only as an almost willful response to the world as he knew it that "The World" has meaning (CCM, 127).

To emphasize this irony, he balanced the cycle "The World" in his 1945 volume *Rescue* with another cycle of poems, "The Voices of Poor People," which were anything but naive. The cycle includes "A Song on the End of the World" and "A Poor Christian Looks at the Ghetto." It also includes bitterly realistic descriptions of Warsaw near the end of the Nazi occupation and poems that question Milosz's own vocation as a poet. In "Song of a Citizen," for instance, he evokes his earlier sense of calling:

> This I wanted and nothing more. In my later years
> like old Goethe to stand before the face of the earth,
> and recognize it and reconcile it
> with my work built up, a forest citadel
> on a river of shifting lights and brief shadows.

But he admits that this is no longer possible:

> This I wanted and nothing more. So who
> is guilty? Who deprived me
> of my youth and my ripe years, who seasoned
> my best years with horror? Who,
> who ever is to blame, who, O God?

This outcry, however, is not just a personal complaint. As he later remembered it, he and his fellow poets were all deeply troubled by profound misgivings: wasn't art in such circumstances immoral? "Poetry, after all, is embedded in the humanistic tradition and is defenseless in the midst of an all-pervading savagery. The very act of writing a poem is an act of faith; yet if screams of the tortured are audible in the poet's room, is not his activity an offense to human suffering?" (HPL, 458). Or as he put it in one of his poems of 1945 during the war, "What is poetry which does not save / Nations or people?" (CP, 78).

To Milosz, the justification for writing poetry in the midst of suffering involved a concrete formulation of the general problem of evil. Moreover, it was a formulation for which his earlier experience as a member of Zagary had particular relevance. Zagary had defined itself against two major currents in Central European poetry. First, its adherents rejected the reduction of poetry to a mere instrument of political change. This was not easy for them because they were socialists. They shared with Marxists a belief in an imminent social catastrophe that would leave their civilization profoundly changed, but they did not believe that this catastrophe was going to initiate a golden age. One of the political polemics in their magazine—also called *Zagary*—admitted that "the times of the great conflagration of accumulated hatred are approaching," but dismissed the Marxist revolutionary expectations as myth: "The myth of the world revolution is flowing, the Communized masses dream of trampling the generation of capitalist bedbugs."[8] If the visionary politics of the Marxists were unacceptable to Zagary, so too was the aestheticism of the earlier generation of Polish poets, the so-called avant garde that used poetry as a retreat from reality and aspired to the formalism of art for art's sake. In *Zagary* Milosz himself wrote a polemic against what he called "those sterile games called pure poetry":

> So is this supposed to be poetry, these poems of yours written not in order to share with people a faith, not in order to praise or condemn, but only to create a combination of images and sound? These poems about which it is impossible to say what concept of the world they serve, or what wisdom they express? Poems which do not come under any definition except that they are badly or cleverly made?" (Carpenter, p. 197)

In Warsaw under the Nazis, Milosz confirmed his sense that poetry was something more than aesthetic play. In his preface to a recent edition of the anti-Nazi anthology he edited during that time, he remarks that people who think of poetry as belonging to a sphere of culture, a vague notion associated with leisure, will find it difficult to understand the role of poetry in the resistance. Poetry then was on the level of essential human needs, like bread, like tools of work and weapons. Poetry was "an affirmation of faith in survival and in victory over the oppressors, also by its very nature, a triumphant manifesto of vitality and a bond between ancestors and descendants" (1S, v–vi).

Yet even in such circumstances Milosz would not permit poetry to be a mere instrument of politics. Hence, in editing his anti-Nazi anthology (an act that could have cost him his life), he faced the same problem he had faced as a member of Zagary, the need to choose between aesthetics and politics—and once again he tried to steer a middle course. As he later said, "I faced a critical problem: a conflict between the detached, almost inhuman standards of art versus un-artistic but profoundly human ethical urges. For, to tell the truth, the most vocal and militant anti-Nazi poems were rather poor artistically, while sophisticated and artistically valid poems . . . were less apt to serve in the combat" (1S, ix). He still rejected poems that were not sufficiently well made.[9] Poetry to him, then, was not so much a weapon as a witness against evil. The writing of poetry affirmed the faith of a people that the world was ultimately good and that lapses into chaos were only temporary. A poem constituted a palpable bond between the quick and the dead. The affirmation of faith could be naive as it was in "The World." But "The Voices of Poor People" suggests the painful context for such a faith. In "The Poor Poet," perhaps the most self-questioning poem in this cycle, Milosz suggests that the burden of witnessing may be too much for the artist to bear.

He begins the poem by evoking his earlier self, the pantheist celebrating nature, a practitioner of the gay science:

> The first movement is singing,
> A free voice, filling mountains and valleys.
> The first movement is joy,
> But it is taken away.   (CP, 60)

This simplicity has been taken away by history, for to continue to write only such paeans would be blasphemy:

> I poise the pen and it puts forth twigs and leaves, it is covered
>   with blossoms
> And the scent of that tree is impudent, for there, on the real
>   earth,
> Such trees do not grow, and like an insult
> To suffering humanity is the scent of that tree.

What is left? Some might be able to use their words as a narcotic for themselves or as propaganda for the state. But these in fact are not real options, nothing Milosz would choose for himself. He must still see himself as that glowing cinder of brushwood, although now his poetry is no longer separated from the suffering it once celebrated. It has become part of that suffering, a way of being punished for having been spared, a way of joining in what accident had spared him:

> But to me a cynical hope is given,
> For since I opened my eyes I have seen only the glow of fires,
>   massacres,
> Only injustice, humiliation, and laughable shame of braggarts.
> To me is given the hope of revenge on others and on myself,
> For I was he who knew
> And took from it no profit for myself.

Poetry is the path of humiliation, or self-revenge, or simple penance. But now the danger was that the suffering of "The Poor Poet" would overwhelm the affirmation of "The World." And this danger was made particularly acute by the ghost of Stanislaw Ignacy Witkiewicz.

This ghost haunted all Polish writers during the war and continued to haunt Milosz long after. ("Haunt" is Milosz's word.) He has admitted that his own literary work during the Nazi occupation, and the work of others as well, was a persistent "polemic with the bleak outlook" of Witkiewicz (HPL, 459). Nor was Witkiewicz a ghost that would be satisfied with a poppy seed world or a few penitential lyrics.

Witkiewicz was so unnerving because he seemed to have fully explored before the war all the meaninglessness that Milosz and his friends experienced during it. Having confronted this meaninglessness, having found no alternative to utter despair, and having seen the war start to confirm his own worst prophecies, Witkiewicz killed himself. Those living through the Nazi occupation of Warsaw felt they owed him an explanation for not following him.[10] And it was uncanny how Witkiewicz anticipated, in particular, Milosz's own cherished answer. Milosz in "The World" would have us recover a childlike wonder at the divine promise within ordinary things. This would reassure us that the Nazi cataclysm was not an expression of the inmost being of things and would therefore pass. But how could Milosz be sure that the childlike awe he so valued was not simple naiveté in the face of reality? How could Milosz be sure that what followed the Nazi horror would not be something even worse?

Already in 1934 Witkiewicz had written a philosophical analysis of the wonder at mere being. He called it "the metaphysical feeling of the strangeness of existence." This feeling comes, Witkiewicz writes, when we ask certain questions: "Why am I exactly this and not that being? at this point of unlimited space and in this moment of infinite time? in this group of beings, on this planet? Why do I exist if I could have been without existence? Why does anything exist at all?" (quoted in HPL, 415). Witkiewicz would have approved of Milosz's preoccupation with the mystery of existence. And surely he would have agreed that the passing of other human beings, such as the hundreds of thousands being killed in Warsaw, was a good focus for meditation on existence—the passing of others and our own survival (for the time being). The metaphysical feeling of the strangeness of existence contains within itself wonder at the instability of human things. In all this Milosz was doing well. But Witkiewicz believed that attempts like Milosz's to find satisfaction in his art were doomed to failure—indeed, were destined only to make matters worse.

Of course men of earlier centuries had sought answers to the mystery of existence. But their religious and philosophical answers, however well they served in the past, no longer sufficed. "Throughout the entire struggle Mystery veils dropped away one by one, and the time has come when we see a naked, hard body with nothing more to be taken off, invincible in its dead statue's indifference" (quoted in HPL, 415). Philosophy is dying, religion already dead. Yet we are left with our metaphysical craving and can only try to satisfy it in art. Yet without some guaranteed ontological foundation for his activity, the artist cannot really satisfy either himself or anyone else. The consequence, for Witkiewicz, was that art could not be an expression of mental health, but a symptom of disease.

Witkiewicz left mankind with but one hope, if it can be called a hope. He experimented widely with drugs, the more mind-altering the better; one result was his nonfictional book, *Nicotine, Alcohol, Cocaine, Peyote, Morphine, Ether*. Since the wonder at existence now results only in anxiety and insanity, what is required is a pill to cure our despair by numbing our capacity to wonder and question. We will then be cured of our humanity and will happily return to mindless bestiality. As Witkiewicz put it, "From a herd we came and to a herd we shall return" (HPL, 416). Witkiewicz at the conclusion of his novel *Insatiability* imagines how the cure might occur. A "Sino-Mongolian" army easily conquers Eastern Europe because of a pill developed by its philosopher, Murti-Bing. Having taken this pill, one no longer worries about unsolvable metaphysical questions; one becomes serene and happy; art, philosophy, and religion are seen as outmoded stupidities; and the advancing Sino-Mongolian army is welcomed with open arms.

Both Witkiewicz in *Insatiability* and Milosz in "A Song for the End of the World" opposed the horrors of history to our wonder at existence. Milosz asserted human wonder as fundamental, the chaos of history secondary. Witkiewicz predicted that history through Murti-Bing or some other spiritual narcotic will finally erase our wonder altogether. During the war Milosz and his fellow Polish poets could face up to the ghost of Witkiewicz. Whatever the death and destruction visited upon the world (and these were far greater than even the sick consciousness of Witkiewicz could imagine), the Nazis would eventually destroy themselves, and the normal goodness of the world would prevail. That Milosz could write poetry like "The World" during the worst part of the Nazi occupation was itself evidence that mindlessness would not triumph. Witkiewicz was wrong when he claimed that religion, philosophy, and art were living out their last days.

Or was he? On September 17, 1939, upon learning that the Red Army had crossed the eastern border of Poland, Witkiewicz committed suicide. Twelve years later, with the Nazis long defeated but the Red Army still in Poland, Czeslaw Milosz, now an ex-diplomat of the People's Republic living in exile in Paris, had to admit that Witkiewicz had proven a true prophet:

> Today Witkiewicz's vision is being fulfilled in the minutest detail throughout a large part of the European continent. Perhaps sunlight, the smell of the earth, little everyday pleasures, and the forgetfulness that work brings can ease somewhat the tensions created by this process of fulfillment. But beneath the activity and bustle of daily life is the constant awareness of an irrevocable choice to be made. One must either die (physically or spiritually), or else one must be reborn according to a prescribed method, namely, the taking of Murti-Bing pills. (CM, 5)

Milosz admitted that history seemed to be going in Witkiewicz's direction. He had to find a new foundation for his pantheistically tinged Christianity and a new justification for his practice as a poet— otherwise there was nothing left except the despair that leads to suicide or drugs. This is the issue to which Milosz in the 1950s devoted himself, and it led him toward the synthesis of *Visions from San Francisco Bay*.

3
Paris

Red fortresses, hazy big cities,
Streams of wings and wires in the sky
Exist for a moment and disintegrate.

So Milosz concluded "A Plain," a poem from his 1945 collection
Rescue.[1] The passage can serve, in its oracular gloom, as a prophecy of
things to come, despite the seeming victory that year over the demonic forces threatening European civilization. He spent the first
years after the war in New York and Washington as a diplomat. His
poems of this period are among his bitterest. The destruction occasioned by World War II was being succeeded by the kind of despair
that Witkiewicz had predicted. And in this spiritual destruction
Milosz, as an official of the People's Republic, was somehow impli-
cated, for he had not yet decided to defect. To make matters worse,
he was stationed in the United States where, as he put it in one poem,
"Nature becomes theater"—that is, where there was little interest in
the sufferings and complexities of Europe that had filled him with
almost inexpressible rage and bitterness (CCM, 152).

The result was a series of poems which he could not work into a larger whole. So *Daylight,* the collection of these intractable poems, Milosz himself has written off as a loss; he explains, "The book's structure is chaotic, because of my difficult personal situation and the pressure of the political atmosphere, which had been alienating me from poetry for a number of years" (CCM, 151). Perhaps most typical of this collection is "Child of Europe":

> We, whose lungs fill with the sweetness of day,
> Who in May admire trees flowering,
> Are better than those who perished.   (CP, 85)

Only the satire of Jonathan Swift was adequate to his situation, and so Milosz lets the people of Europe describe themselves in Swiftian terms. These children of the European experience can boast of having saved themselves by their own "cunning and knowledge":

> By sending others to the more exposed positions,
> Urging them loudly to fight on,
> Ourselves withdrawing in certainty of the cause lost.

Now that they have survived, the Europeans can go about the business of rewriting history to glorify themselves and consign the idealistic—"the gullible, hot-blooded weaklings, careless with their lives"—to oblivion.

> Grow your tree of falsehood from a small grain of truth.
> Do not follow those who lie in contempt of reality.
> Let your lie be even more logical than the truth itself,
> So the weary travelers may find repose in the lie.

The specific historical context for this poem is the Stalinist reinterpretation of the Warsaw uprising. Milosz in his *Collected Poems* of 1988 still feels he must provide a historical gloss for American readers:

> The Warsaw Uprising broke out on August 1, 1944, when the victorious Soviet Army was approaching the city and the German army was retreating. The battles in the city—between the German army and Polish fighters—raged for over two months, and as a result Warsaw

was totally destroyed. The insurgents, who were not pro-Soviet, were subsequently accused of being fascists. (CP, 495)

So his "Mid-Twentieth-Century Portrait," which he yokes with "Child of Europe" as his most important poetry of this period, portrays one of the new Polish commissars as a bundle of self-canceling contradictions and hypocrisies:

> Keeping one hand on Marx's writings, he reads the Bible in
>   private.
> His mocking eye on processions leaving burned-out churches.
> His backdrop: a horseflesh-colored city in ruins.
> In his hand: a memento of a boy "fascist" killed in the
>   Uprising.   (CP, 90)

This is a world in which whole cities fall into ruin; this is a civilization in which the victor's lies can deny the ruins, and are driven to do so by what passes now for civilization in Europe. So in "Earth" Milosz mockingly praises his "sweet European homeland":

> You are a land where it's no shame to suffer
> For one is served here a glass of bitter liquor
> With lees, the poison of centuries.   (CP 105)

But is poison the sole product of civilization? He yearns for a poetry that protects the truth and is still uncorrupted by the cynical mendacity. He writes in "You Who Wronged":

> Do not feel safe. The poet remembers.
> You can kill one, but another is born.
> The words are written down, the deed, the date.   (CP 106)

In "Spirit of the Laws" his anger seems directed not just against Europe and its poison of centuries, but against nature itself:

> And I, with my pine anchor on a sandy plain,
> With the silenced memory of dead friends
> And the silenced memory of towns and rivers,
> I was ready to tear out the heart of the earth with a knife
> And put there a glowing diamond of shouts and complaints.
>   (CP 100)

Not only was history going Witkiewicz's way; Milosz was too. His rage at his impotence was such that it could scarcely be sanely sustained. It is hard not to think that he identifies his own poetry with the broken pieces in his "Song of Porcelain," shards found in the ruins of Warsaw, "pretty, useless foam," "bits of brittle froth":

> Of all things broken and lost
> Porcelain troubles me most . . .
> In the mounds of these new graves.
> In sorrow and pain and cost,
> Sir, porcelain troubles me most.   (CP, 83)

Readers of the poems in *Daylight* will not find it surprising to learn that Milosz felt his own poetic powers to be deserting him. One of his poems is a prayer for the end of this poetically dry period of Swiftian rage. "Mittelbergheim" pleads, "Do not yet force me to open my lips. / Let me trust and believe I will attain" (CP, 107). What he wants to believe is that poetry is still in him, but "it is too early, let the wine mature." He later referred to this poem as one of convalescence. The beginning of this recovery was Milosz's defection to the west in Paris in 1951. The next step was to refute Witkiewicz's vision of the future; this he did in *The Captive Mind*, the first book written in exile and perhaps still his best-known work.[2]

Milosz began his new book by conceding that Witkiewicz had been right to claim that, in the new dispensation, social organisms would be transformed into abstract Molochs and intellectuals would serve as priests. Still he believed that Witkiewicz had underestimated the resourcefulness of our species, its sly waterlike flowing around obstacles that are but a frozen vestige of our creative powers. Milosz insists that his western readers understand that for him and for other Central Europeans the war was a test of reality, not an aberration to be forgotten as quickly as possible. "Which world is 'natural'? That which existed before, or the world of war? Both are natural, if both are within the realm of one's experience. All the concepts men live by are a product of the historic formation in which they find themselves. Fluidity and constant change are the characteristics of phenomena" (CM, 28–29). In recognizing this fluidity we experience the strangeness of existence in its most acute form, as spiritual terror. Only after feeling that spiritual terror ourselves can we understand why the totalitarian states of Central Europe did not lack for intellectuals to serve them. The war revealed the radical instability of life and the emptiness at the heart of human things; traditional philosophy and religion failed to explain away this apparent chaos—people looking within themselves found exactly nothing; they were ready for the pill of Murti-Bing. But Milosz continues to insist that this nihilism is not a permanent part of the human condition, but only the law of our times.

If he felt only emptiness inside him, "Dante could not have written his *Divine Comedy,* or Montaigne his Essays, nor Chardin have painted a single still-life." Witkiewicz claimed that faith in oneself was becoming an impossibility. Milosz, in choosing exile, was gambling that Witkiewicz was wrong. He was gambling that the radical mutations that religion, philosophy, and art were undergoing in the twentieth century need not be equated with their disappearance. "Suppose one can live without outside pressure, suppose one can create one's own inner tension—then it is not true that there is nothing in man. To take this risk would be an act of faith" (77).

Of course Milosz in exile was already taking that risk, and faith was the right word. He admitted that his decision had not been a rational one: "My own decision proceeded not from the functioning of the reasoning mind, but from a revolt of the stomach" (xii). Through this physical revolt Milosz was going to try to find something within himself, something more than a function of social forces. He wanted to find within himself what Dante would have called his soul, Montaigne his self—and what Chardin had sought even in inanimate things. Milosz could not quite yet say what he was seeking; he could not quite say why he had chosen to defect. But he knew that, if ever he could say it, he would be a wise man. As he tried to explain to himself why, his mind rested on one incident from the past.

In my wanderings at the beginning of the Second World War, I happened to find myself, for a very short while, in the Soviet Union. I was waiting for a train at a station in one of the large cities of the Ukraine . . . As I was passing through the station I suddenly stopped and looked. A peasant family—husband and wife and two children— had settled down by the wall. They were sitting on baskets and bundles. The wife was feeding the younger child; the husband, who had a dark, wrinkled face and black, drooping mustache, was pouring tea out of a kettle into a cup for the other boy. They were whispering to each other in Polish. I gazed at them until I felt moved to the point of tears. What had stopped my steps so suddenly and touched me so profoundly was their *difference*. This was a human group, an island in a crowd that lacked something proper to humble, ordinary human life. The gesture of a hand pouring tea, the careful, delicate handing of the cup to the child, the worried words I guessed from the movement of their lips, their isolation, their privacy in the midst of the crowd—that is what moved me. For a moment, then, I understood something that quickly slipped from my grasp. (248–249)

However striking this scene, the reader may be perplexed as to why Milosz attaches so much importance to it, especially when it is left unclear what exactly he had grasped momentarily. Milosz's response to the scene—and much else that is initially enigmatic about *The Captive Mind*—becomes comprehensible if we look at it in reference to Simone Weil, who at this point in Milosz's development became something like a patron saint—or rather a guardian angel to save him from the temptations of Witkiewicz.

Milosz's reading of Weil began in the late 1940s when he was still a Polish cultural attaché in Washington, struggling with the decision to defect. In the 1950s he edited and translated into Polish Weil's selected works. Finally, in 1960 he explained her influence on him in an essay, "The Importance of Simone Weil" (EE, 85–98).

Through Weil, Milosz came to realize that the problem so vexing to him and the rest of his era was the old problem of evil: "Who can justify the suffering of the innocent?" The predicament of the mid-

twentieth century, which Witkiewicz wanted to claim was unprecedented, was at least as old as the Book of Job. Weil's own response to
the predicament was essentially religious.

In 1938, five years before her death at the age of thirty-five (she was
only three years older than Milosz), Weil had a mystical experience.
An atheist all her life, she was, in her own phrase, "captured by
Christ." But this did not lead her to conventional Christianity; she
found her religion within her atheism. "Religion, in so far as it is a
source of consolation, is a hindrance to true faith; in this sense
atheism is a purification. I have to be an atheistic with that part of
myself which is not made for God. Among those in whom the
supernatural part of themselves has not been awakened, the atheists
are right and the believers wrong."[3] How could God permit a world
like ours to exist? Weil's answer is no simple consolation. God, to
permit the universe to exist, had to withdraw from it, and he thereby
committed all phenomena without exception to the mechanisms of
the world. Weil, therefore, is as deterministic as any Marxist—only
she regards necessity as God's veil.

But how do we know that something lies behind the veil? How do
we know that Witkiewicz is wrong when he contends that, after we
have stripped away the last veil of being and gaze at what is left, we
will be driven insane? Weil would have us focus on the contradiction
between the necessity that governs the world and the good that
governs our ideals. The distance between the necessary and the good
is the same distance as that between the creature and the Creator.
This contradiction between the good and the true is for Weil the lever
of transcendence. How can we be sure that this postulation of the
good behind the true is not itself a delusion? The assurance is aesthetic. In contemplating necessity we find that it is the indirect
manifestation of something infinitely greater because it is beautiful.
The absence of God becomes for Weil the most marvelous testimony
of perfect love; and that is why pure necessity, manifestly different
from the good, is beautiful.

The beautiful is somehow the mediation between the true and the
good. In finding beauty in tragic necessities inseparable from the

human condition (which is precisely what the greatest artists do), we are loving the God who is absent. "To love God through and across the destruction of Troy and Carthage and without consolation. Love is not consolation, it is light." Milosz, as he thought back through his life, realized he had experienced the pure love of good once, in that Soviet railway station. Simone Weil had taught him to recognize this light for what it was.

It would be hard to overestimate the importance of Weil for Milosz as he was writing *The Captive Mind*. Indeed, the very title seems to have been taken from one of Weil's last essays, "Human Personality" (published posthumously in 1950). In this essay Weil maintains that there is something sacred at the center of every human being—and this sacred center is not the personality, that combination of attitudes and habits produced by historical circumstances. No, it is divine spark, an impersonal core that enables human beings to produce Gregorian chant, Romanesque architecture, the *Iliad*: "The people through whom they were brought into being and made available to us [did not regard them as] occasions for the manifestation of personality." Those who are unaware of this inner spark are reduced to considering themselves the products of social forces. And they are trapped in language, as captive minds:

> At the very best, a mind enclosed in language is in prison . . . If a captive mind is unaware of being in prison, it is living in error. If it has recognized the fact, even for the tenth of a second, and then quickly forgotten it in order to avoid suffering, it is living in falsehood. Men of the most brilliant intelligence can be born, live, and die in error and falsehood. In them, intelligence is neither a good nor even an asset. The difference between more or less intelligent men is like the difference between criminals condemned to life imprisonment in smaller or larger cells. The intelligent man who is proud of his intelligence is like a condemned man who is proud of his large cell. (330–331)

The Captive Mind reads like a demonstration of Weil's thesis, especially the middle four chapters. These give portraits of four captives who are proud of the size of their Soviet cells. Each had traded his past for the illusory advantage of power that ideology proffered them; each had transformed, in that exchange, weakness into an apparent strength; and each was doomed to loose his soul in the bargain, as Milosz, their friend in cynical bitterness, could so easily have: "Human sufferings are drowned in the trumpet-blare: the orchestra in the concentration camp; and I, as a poet, had my place already marked out for me among the first violins" (x).

This small gallery of mordantly drawn prisoners of ideology is of a piece with Milosz's bitter poetry of the late forties, such as "Child of Europe" and "Mid-Twentieth-Century Portrait." The only difference is that Milosz no longer numbers himself among the captives. For Paul Coates, a perceptive reader of Milosz's work of the period, this is what makes *The Captive Mind* such a fascinating and disturbing book—the "grim self-satisfaction" with which he castigates others.[4]

Certainly Milosz is justifying his own decision to defect; and the obvious implication is that this puts him in a superior moral position. What this criticism of the book misses, however, is Milosz's own account of why he was saved from the captivity that engulfs the others. From the very beginning he insists that his choice to defect was more a visceral matter than one of intellect or will; his decision was, as we have noted, a "revolt of the stomach." But what was it that gave him such a queasy stomach?

Milosz was saved because he had once recognized he was living in error. This, as Weil taught him, was the significance of the episode in the train station. Not that he had then embraced the experience—he had in fact done the opposite, trying his best to forget it in order to avoid suffering. So he had for a time managed to live superficially, in New York, Washington, Warsaw, Paris, writing less and less poetry, with what he did write becoming more and more bitter, until finally he could stand it no longer. Simone Weil in her essay describes what happens next:

> A man whose mind feels that it is captive would prefer to blind himself to the fact. But if he hates falsehood, he will not do so; and in that case he will have to suffer a lot. He will beat his head against the wall until

he faints. He will come to again and look with terror at the wall, until one day he begins afresh to beat his head against it; and once again he will faint. And so on endlessly and without hope. One day he will wake up on the other side of the wall. Perhaps he is still in a prison, although a larger one. No matter. He has found the key; he knows the secret which breaks down every wall. He has passed beyond what men call intelligence, into the beginning of wisdom. (331)

What Milosz could never stop seeking was the other side of the wall. What he had found by 1953 was the beginning of wisdom.[5]

We must see beauty as the mediation between necessity and the good, between gravity and grace. Milosz tried to expand this theme in the book he wrote immediately after *The Captive Mind: The Seizure of Power*. This was a hastily written novel, designed—successfully, as it turned out—to win a literary contest. So it is far from Milosz's best work—in fact, he does not even mention it among his prose works in *History of Polish Literature*. Nonetheless, as Milosz tells this story of the Nazi occupation of Warsaw, he also sometimes shows us how far his own understanding of the artistic vocation has deepened since the war, how far he has come since writing the bitter "The Poor Poet."

> The wind carried the smoke from the burning ghetto toward the churches from which people were issuing, wearing their Sunday clothes, chattering, and moving through the fair grounds where girls' dresses fluttered on merry-go-rounds. Old women were saying anxiously: "They're burning the Jews now. It will be our turn next." Here, in that space, was the memory of a hundred deaths, of two hundred thousand deaths, of five hundred thousand deaths—each different, individual, interrupting a different love, a different desire, a different hope. Now, in the autumn sunshine, the wormwood—its root embedded in greasy ashes, in clots of earth, fertilized by blood—waved in the breeze. (TSP, 57)

What Weil would have admired about this passage is its aspiration to Homeric impersonality, to a beauty in which life is not a consolation but a light.

The central character of the novel crosses the Russian frontier in order to live under the Nazis, as Milosz himself actually did. He describes his character's motives:

> At the time he refused to admit the reason to himself—a desire to be purified, to atone, to share the misfortunes of a humiliated people. He cherished, too, the completely irrational hope that from the chaos something new would emerge one day, something with a better, still undefined shape. But these motives were overshadowed by a great and, as it seemed to him, egotistical desire: to reorganize himself, to have plenty of time, to place himself somewhere outside official life where he could begin everything over again, where thought was free precisely because it was entirely prohibited. (17)

This is a captive mind deluding itself. It cherishes the nineteenth-century dream in progress, with fascism as perhaps the last and necessary stage of capitalism. But it also worships its own personality, a catastrophist personality that seeks an occasion to renew itself. Yet behind all this delusion there is grace, an unconscious motive to be purified through suffering and humiliation and thereby to become aware of the sacred.

This character, like Milosz, will survive the Nazi regime, will try to work within the new Russian-dominated government, and eventually will defect to the west to start his life over once again. But we don't know whether he has yet achieved wisdom. There is one character in *The Seizure of Power* who does achieve wisdom: Professor Gil, whose postwar meditations begin and end the novel. Gil has lost his wife and only child in the war. He has been removed from his position at the university by the Communists and survives on the pittance they provide him for translating Thucydides. He is contemptuously dismissed by the younger Poles for his petty-bourgeois mentality. So the professor is left in peace to go about his task of translation. He has gotten as far as the plague in Athens that would sweep away Pericles and much of the Athenian promise. It is not in Gil's power to save Pericles, any more than it was in his power to save his own family. But he can try "by using the full power of the imagination" to recreate "the gestures of a sorrowing Athenian woman, the expression on the face of a man looking at his dead son, the unique, inimitable shape of fingers holding a jar of wine." If he can do this, then time would be overcome: "There would be only a great coexistence of a countless number of separate human beings, who had been and who were yet to be each communicating to the other the same complaint" (241). Professor Gil has reached his highest wisdom.

Milosz comments: "He who would be equal to the human condition must collect blood in a basin without spilling a single drop—not to prove that all knowledge was possessed already and to transform heartbreak to indifference but, on the contrary, to preserve the gifts of anger and of unbreakable faith" (242). From one perspective such a task seemed meaningless, something that would be lost amid "the mass of human endeavors and strivings." Nonetheless, when Gil was absorbed in translating, he felt all who once were to be near him, and he was "warmed by their breath and communion with them brought peace." Perhaps he had found an answer to "the only important question: how a man could preserve himself from the taint of sadness or indifference" (245). But perhaps the affirmation of Gil, value bearer in a novel written for money, is come by too easily and seems a little sentimental. And perhaps Gil is also too far away from the experience of his creator.

Although Milosz has always regarded *The Seizure of Power* as a potboiler, he treats his second novel and last, *The Issa Valley,* with respect, even affection. Part of the explanation is biographical. If, as he later said, a poem like "Mittelbergheim" is a work of poetic convalescence, *Issa Valley* marked the first important step back from the bitterness of *Daylight* to the kind of poetry he felt to be his true calling. No wonder then that Milosz wrote, "*Issa Valley* is a novel close to the very core of Milosz' poetry." He adds: "It has been called 'pagan' because of its childish amazement with the world; but this story of childhood in Lithuania, with its simple images of nature, is somewhat deceptive, as underneath lurks a Manichean vision" (HPL, 529).

Here we have the two poles of Milosz's work—pantheism and Christianity—represented in new form, as affected by Simone Weil. Weil showed Milosz how to combine his earlier pantheistic awe with the preoccupations forced on him by his experience of the war and its aftermath. The two poles, it seems, could be reconciled only through a heretical form of Christianity, Manicheanism, which Weil herself embraced.[6]

If Milosz were to follow the Marxists, he must elevate history and use dialectical materialism to explain away evil as a personal delusion. If he were to follow Witkiewicz, he must deem any good he experiences in nature a delusion, masking the essential absurdity of the human condition. As a Manichean, he can at once admit that the world is ruled by necessity, by evil, and yet still find hope and sustenance in the beauty of the world. History reveals the pointlessness of human striving, the instability of human things; but time also is the moving image of eternity.

It is strange that so many of its readers have missed the serious Manichean theme in *Issa Valley*—and not just because it is so elaborately developed there.[7] Anyone coming to *Issa Valley* from *The Captive Mind* should see the obvious connection between the novel and the last chapter of the political tract, "The Lesson of the Baltics," on the fate of Lithuania, Estonia, and Latvia. What happened to these countries under Stalin was as bad as what happened to Warsaw and the Jews under Hitler.

Readers have to realize that the pastoral way of life recorded in *Issa Valley* is doomed and will be violently swept away in less than a human lifetime after the events narrated in the novel. How should we respond to the life of *Issa Valley*? With pagan delight, with a simple assent? Yes, this is how humans should live, it is the best they can hope for. The more readers say yes to this way of life, and the more they find of beauty and humanity there, then the more they will be repulsed at the fate of these people, and the more they will experience the distance between the true and the good—and the closer they will come to the Manichean vision. One needs no knowledge of Lithuanian history to be led toward this position, for the Manichean point is built into the very structure of the novel. It tells the story of the childhood and coming of age of Thomas. The dialectical structure is already found in the two prefatory sections before the introduction of the boy.

The first section (of the seventy into which the book is divided) celebrates the beauty of Issa Valley, of which the ordinary life of its human inhabitants is no small part. It begins:

> The Issa is a deep, black river with a lazy current, thickly bordered with reeds; a river whose surface is barely visible in places under the lily pads, which winds through meadows and between gentle slopes noted for their fecundity. The Valley is blessed with an abundance of black earth—a rarity for us—with the lushness of its orchards, and possibly with its remoteness from the world, something that has never seemed to bother its inhabitants. (5)

This beauty, however, is only one aspect of the valley. Section two begins: "The Issa Valley has the distinction of being inhabited by an unusually large number of devils" (6). However slyly expressed, this is no joke, either for the residents of the valley or for the narrator. The residents, simply, naively, believe in these devils. We may in our sophistication dismiss them, but Milosz challenges sophistication with Lithuanian belief, which he never patronizes. The presence of devils amid the beauty of the valley constitutes the central metaphysical problem of *Issa Valley,* the problem of evil.

The Lithuanians are not quite so naive in their demonology as we might at first expect. They sometimes call the demons "Little Germans." Germans for them are quintessentially people of progress, people of commerce, science, technology. The residents of Issa Valley sense that the devil is also on the side of progress (and that progress threatens everything they hold dear). The demons have always wanted to destroy Issa Valley, but the residents have managed to hold them at bay. They know that progress, history, can give the demons a chance to do unprecedented damage. Thus the central issue of Issa Valley is twofold. There is the traditional problem of evil: what are demons doing in this beautiful world? Then there is the new variation on the old problem: what is the relation of the demons to people like the Germans who seem to embody the forces of progress?

> Are the devils and those other creatures joined in a pact, or do they simply exist side by side like the jay, the sparrow, and the cow? And where is that realm where both species would take refuge when the earth was plowed up by the tracks of tanks; when those who were about to be executed dug their own shallow graves by the river; and when, in blood and tears, Industrialization rose up, surrounded by the halo of History? (7)

The people of Issa Valley have no doubt as to the correct answer to the second question; they would treat a German with the same superstitious awe as they would a demon. Nor would Simone Weil have any doubt as to the correct answer. She believed that man in a state of nature was oppressed by its power. This oppression provided the motivation for social organization, division of labor, technology, and the like. The increasing control over the forces of nature required that social organization and the instruments of technology themselves become larger and larger, until finally they are so large that they are no longer under human control: they submit large portions of humanity to an oppression more complete than can be found in nature itself. They become a second nature more ruthless than first nature itself; these demons were not indifferent. This seems to be Milosz's vision as well.

> One can easily imagine a parliamentary session being convened in caverns deep inside the earth, so deep that it is warmed by the fires of the earth's molten center. The session is attended by hundreds of thousands of tiny devils in frock coats, who listen solemnly to speakers representing the Central Committee of Infernos. The speakers announce that, in the interest of the cause, all dancing in the forests and meadows will have to cease; that from now on, highly qualified specialists will have to operate in such a way that the minds of mortals will never suspect their presence. There is applause but it is strained, for those present realize that they were necessary only during the prepara-

tory stage, that progress has consigned them to gloomy chasms, and that they will never again witness the setting of the sun, the flight of kingfishers, the glitter of stars, and all the other wonders of the uncircumscribable earth. (7)

The old demons are clearly not as bad as the new one. The old demons were tiny persons, the new one is the gigantic, impersonal collectivity of a central committee. And the earlier demons were never far from the wondrous beauty of nature, while now they have to haunt chasms no better than steel mills.

The dualism announced in the first two sections of *Issa Valley* is continued throughout the rest. Section three introduces us to Thomas within the context of the beautiful valley: "Thomas was born in the village of Gine at that time of year when a ripe apple thumps to the ground during the afternoon lull and when vats of freshly brewed ale stand in the hallway after the autumnal harvest. Gine was not much more than a hill, thickly wooded with oaks" (8). Gine might appear little more than a hill, but it is a town and therefore contains lurking demons of history. Thomas might seem just a simple baby, but he too is, at least in part, a creature of history. And so section four presents Thomas to us from the contrary perspective of historical demonics: "Thomas's ancestors belonged to the landowning gentry . . . They had worn helmets and swords, and the local villagers had been forced to work in their fields" (11). There had been revolts and massacres, a time when grain was exported to Niemen, a time of prosperity and brutal class divisions—but all that is past now. Issa is in decline, its history largely forgotten, and hence its idyllic appearance. Again and again Milosz will create a beautiful surface, only to move down to the demons that lurk beneath.

Thomas enters this world of Issa with a childish sense of wonder. He wakes "on a summer morning to the oriole's song outside his window, to a chorus of quacks, cackling, and gaggling from the barnyard, to a steady stream of voices bathed in never-ending light . . . Touch was also a kind of ecstasy—the feel of naked feet racing over smooth boards onto the cool of a corridor's tiled floor, over a garden path's circular flagstone still wet with dew." Thomas, however inno-cent he may be, is not alone in his world, for there are powers watching him who "shake their diaphanous heads in dismay, for they could foresee the effects of the ecstatic state in which he lived." The devils have plans for Thomas, but they must proceed carefully. So they play a waiting game, and even Thomas seems unaware of their presence: "Devils, rapidly shrinking and taking cover under leaves at the sound of footsteps, were forever imitating hens when, all aflutter, they crane their necks and reveal a moronic look in their eye" (19).

These chicken-devils are the little natural demons that the residents have been living with for centuries—but there are larger demonic forces at work on the fringes of Issa Valley. The European world is involved in a Great War, and the czar has to retreat before advancing Germans. So remote is Issa Valley that Thomas sees the Germans only once, and then it is only three of them who stop for a moment at Gine to get a drink of water before mounting up again. The boy holds one young officer in awe: "Thomas all but fell in love with his agility, and with something else not quite definable" (3). Remember-ing the connection made earlier between Germans and demons, the reader might well think this childish admiration something that Thomas will outgrow. As if to emphasize just this, Milosz adds an aside after pointing out that the young German officer does not notice the admiring Thomas:

> He never noticed Thomas, not then or—why not?—twenty years la-ter as he sat in a general's car, surrounded by comfortable rugs and thermos bottles, his corpulent chin propped against the collar of his uniform, and was chauffeured through the streets of an East European city freshly conquered by the Fuhrer's army. Clenching his fists in his pockets (we can assume he did), Thomas refused to recognize in the conqueror the object of his short-lived affection. (31)

So we are informed that Thomas as an adult, after confronting the forces of history at their most demonic, will not be reduced to sadness and indifference. He, like Professor Gil, will have the capacity for anger and perhaps even hope. We know, then, that Thomas' growing up in Issa Valley will be a success.

The story of Thomas' adjustment to this Manichean world is framed by two human failures. Magdalena, a young housekeeper who becomes pregnant by her priest, has to be sent away but cannot submit and kills herself by taking rat poison. Even in death she does not accept her fate, and so her ghost continues to haunt the village until the villagers dig up her corpse to put a stake through her heart. But she still does not entirely submit; she persists in haunting Thomas in dream, in memory, in imagination. One dream in particular he can never forget:

> He saw Magdalena in the earth, in the solitude of the immense earth, where she had been dwelling for years and would go on dwelling forever. Her dress had rotted away, shreds of cloth had merged with dry bones, while the strand of hair that used to slip down over her cheek as she bent over the kitchen stove was not stuck fast to her skull . . . "Oh, why must I fade, why must my arms and legs fade away? Why am I alive, yet not alive—I, who once lived, just once, from the beginning till the end of the world? Oh, the sky and the sun will still be there when I am long gone. Only these bones will be left . . . Oh, nothing, nothing is mine." (57–58)

Balthasar is the second failure, and he is an imposing presence of flesh and blood whose sorry tale is spread out over the whole length of the novel. The dualism of the novel is contained in the sentence that introduces Balthasar to the reader: "If anyone was hounded by devils, it was Balthasar, even though he had the look of a man born for joy" (34). The beauty of this sentence, even in English, is that Balthasar, this latterday wiseman, is suspended in the middle between the devils who hound him and the joy for which he has been born.

Although he began as a simple forester, Balthasar has become a well-to-do man. He even has a house with a plank floor and four outbuildings. He has married into a prosperous family. And he is respected for the discretion with which he acts. So he sits on his front porch with a jug of homemade beer beside him, stretched out like a contented cat. Yet Balthasar is not a cat but a man, and thereby conscious of the dualities of this world. And so he is, at the very moments he should be most enjoying his animal comforts, given to fits of metaphysical depression. He does have something to be dissatisfied with: his wife is very ugly. And he does have something to feel guilty about: he had once, for no apparent reason, shot and killed an escaped prisoner of war who was crossing Balthasar's land in a desperate effort to return home. These two things Balthasar slowly broods into a metaphysical problem.

Toward the middle of the novel, Balthasar seeks out the wisest man of the region, the famous Rabbi of Silelai, for help with his problem, but the rabbi will not listen to his story and instead advises him: "Whatever wrong you have committed, man, that and only that is your fate. Do not curse your fate, man, for whoever thinks he has another and not his own is lost and will be damned forever. Think not of the life that might have been, for such a life would not have been yours" (154). At first Balthasar is furious at the advice—"no angels, no trumpets, no fiery tongues, no swords forked like fangs"— but finally on reflection he becomes bitterly morose and goes back to his beer. The next time we see Balthasar, he is drunk, and his metaphysical torment has worsened: "It's not enough! Not enough! It was not just enough to live! . . . It's all wrong! All wrong" (233). He now is no longer protesting the specifics of his own life, but the limitations of any life in this world.

Finally, near the end of the novel, Balthasar goes berserk, destroying his own farm, killing a neighbor, only to be mortally wounded himself, slowly dying but refusing the consolations of the priest: "Nothing can save me" (264). Milosz explains that this was all "Balthasar's eternal protest—against the law which leaves nothing alone but chains us to its consequences" (257). Thus Balthasar, like Magdelena (who would not submit to the consequences of her sin and then not even to her own death), is damned. He had, in Weil's terms, refused the extreme and total humiliation which is also the condition of passing over into truth. He prefers death and damnation to any abnegation of pride.

Thomas succeeds where Balthasar fails. His education has truly begun when he experiences the duality of good and evil within nature. Thomas has a particular devotion to birds and finds contradiction in contemplating a pet owl, who is at once pet and predator; then he finds it within himself, a lover of birds who also loves to hunt them. "The truth was that Thomas hungered for a sort of impossible communion with living creatures. Why this barrier, and why become a hunter if one loved nature?" (176). Once he finds duality within his own breast, he begins to regard the human condition as pitiable:

> For the first time he perceived that he had two selves, and that they were not altogether commensurate: the one he felt inside, and the outside one, his bodily self, the one he was born with, and nothing of which was really his . . . We live inside ourselves as in a prison. If people make fun of us, it's because they can't see through to our true selves. We carry inside images of our physical selves closely bound to our souls, though all it takes is another person's glance to dissolve that bond, to show us that we are not at all what we flatter ourselves to be. Chastened, we go around, existing inside ourselves, all too painfully aware of ourselves from the outside. (180–181)

This duality, this sense of being a captive mind, finally becomes so great that it produces a crisis:

> God, let me be like the others—Thomas prayed, and the demons, plotting their next move, strained to listen. Make me a good shot with a gun, don't let me forget my hunter's, naturalist's vow. Cure me of that illness (a loud guffawing among the baser demons along the Issa, of which there were a great many). Let me understand your world when it pleases you to enlighten. The way it really is, not what I imagine it to be (here the demons fell to sulking, for the topic had turned grave). (249)

The devils are sulking because Thomas has submitted to necessity and is thereby saved from the bitterness and despair that destroys

Magdelena and Balthasar. He has survived the demons of nature and is now ready to confront the demons of history.

As there is a pair who defy necessity and damn themselves, so *Issa Valley* also contains a pair who submit successfully to necessity, but only because they are unaware of the questions that trouble Thomas and destroy Balthasar. There is Romauld, who Thomas admires for his hunting skill. Romauld has aspirations to marry Thomas' aunt, but he also has more immediate needs that are met by his servant girl Barbarka. Eventually he finds himself maneuvered into marrying the girl, and he submits to this necessity without a murmur, just as he has always been aware of his limitations when on the hunt.

This kind of wisdom, an uncomplaining submission to necessity, is also personified in Thomas' Grandmother Misia. Just before Balthasar suffers his final breakdown, we hear Milosz's assessment of the grandmother:

> Grandmother Misia was the epitome of serenity. Rocked by the waves of a mighty river, she lived in a perpetual hush of timeless waters. If birth was a passage from the protection of the maternal womb into a world of sharp, wounding objects, then Grandmother Misia had never been born, having always existed, wrapped in the silk cocoon of that which Is . . . and the only prayer she ever required was one that could be reduced to a single, incantatory, "Oh." (253)

Grandmother Diblin, Thomas' pious grandmother, always dismisses Misia as "that pagan." And Milosz agrees. "Mindful of her place in the infinite, caressed by a giant hand, she is content to purr" (254). It might be thought that Milosz himself is advocating such a condition. He admits that the demons have long since given up on Misia: "There was no attacking the innocent, those never burdened by the awareness of sin" (254). Indeed, shortly before the conclusion of *Issa Valley*, Milosz seems explicitly to advocate this paganism.

A first child is born to Romauld and Barbarka (six months after marriage):

> The thaw wind came from the west, from the sea. Out there were ships, pitching and sounding their horns as they plied waters between the

shores of Sweden and Finland, between the Hanseatic city of Riga and Hanseatic Danzig. But here was Barbarka, changing her son's diapers, holding him by the ankles and lightly tilting the little fanny that always roused her to such tenderness. Such sentiments, like those she had when she offered her son her blue-veined breast, were not to be transposed beyond the realm of experience proper to them. We are given to live on the border of the human and bestial, and it is good so. (283–284)

It is good so—and thus a page later, when Thomas and his mother load up their wagon to leave Issa Valley, we are meant to be sad. Still we should not envy those who remain in Issa Valley, or rather not aspire for a return to that condition. We, like Thomas, know sin and hence cannot (anymore than Balthasar could) purr contentedly like a cat.

Moreover, we are indirectly reminded that the residents of Issa Valley are not going to be left alone for much longer. Between the scene of Barbarka's nursing her baby and the scene of Thomas and his mother leaving in the wagon, there intrudes a page describing someone new, Dominic Malinowski. Why introduce a new character when the novel is almost finished? This is a man as angry with the world as Balthasar is. But Dominic has been given a focus for his hate. His mother was forever talking to him about land reform: "They are parceling it out everywhere" (285). Dominic, who knew better, would only play with his knife and brood. This is Milosz's way of reminding us that one day, with a man like Dominic as commissar, all the land of Issa Valley will be parceled out and the way of life Milosz has so lovingly detailed will end.

Thomas is leaving the valley, going out into the broader world to see the great demons that control history. The baby of Barbarka will not have to. By the time he is Thomas' age, the forces of history will themselves be coming into Issa Valley.

In *The Captive Mind, The Seizure of Power,* and *The Issa Valley,* Milosz was writing as a Weilian. If this is an exaggeration, it is only a slight one. By 1958, however, when his translations of Weil into Polish first appear, he has already begun to see the limitations of her thought. His admiration for her is still almost without limits, but he did not have her mystical temperament. He could not contemplate directly the transcendent realm. As he put it, "I consider myself a Caliban, too fleshy, too heavy, to take on the feathers of Ariel. Simone Weil was an Ariel." One of his poems of this period is on precisely this theme:

> Come, Holy Spirit,
> bending or not bending the grasses,
> appearing or not above our heads in a tongue of flame,
> at hay harvest or when they plow in the orchards or when snow
> covers crippled firs in the Sierra Nevada.
> I am only a man: I need visible signs.
> I tire easily, building the stairway of abstraction.
> Many a time I asked, you know it well, that the statue in church
> lift its hand, only once, just once, for me.
> But I understand that signs must be human,
> therefore call one man, anywhere on earth,
> not me—after all I have some decency—
> and allow me, when I look at him, to marvel at you.   (CP, 194)

Weil would have wanted the Holy Spirit to come; she would have wished for that direct experience. (Or rather she did not have to wish because she actually had a mystical experience.) Milosz has no such hopes. He is still Caliban, someone who needs visible signs, someone who tires easily and cannot climb stairways of abstraction. If he is to experience God, it will have to be within the things of this world. He prays that he can experience the deity through the mediation of another human being—"and allow me, when I look at him, to marvel at you." But this Caliban did have his prayer answered, twice: first in the Soviet train station and then in the writings of Simone Weil.

Milosz is, in effect, reasserting the conclusion of his wartime cycle, "The World." He will not attempt to look at the sun directly; he will observe it only as it is reflected in smaller things. But Milosz now knows that if he is not to be a pure Weilian or revert to the atheism of Witkiewicz, he must develop his own justification for his art; he must develop his own aesthetics.

Milosz had in fact done just that in a long poem, *Treatise on Poetry*, finished in 1957. In his preface he explains the need for poetry. People feel slightly ashamed when they look through a book of poems because they think poetry itself has become a secondary activity, mere verbal entertainment and buffoonery:

> Seasoned with jokes, clowning, satire,
> Poetry still knows how to please.
> Then its excellence is much admired.
> But the grave combats where life is at stake
> Are fought in prose. It was not always so.

It was not always so and, despite appearances, is not now. Thus the polemical stance of the preface:

> Novels and essays serve but will not last.
> One clear stanza can take more weight
> Than a whole wagon of elaborate prose.   (CP, 111)

"Weight" is the key word here—it is exactly what Weil would contrast with grace. Weight ties us to the material in our search for spiritual transcendence.

Milosz's aesthetics, like Weil's philosophy, is grounded in contradiction. But he does not use contradiction as the lever of transcendence, as a way of reaching up to the Holy Spirit. He uses it as a lever of immanence, as a way of getting to the divine *within* things. This is Caliban's response to Ariel. Milosz of course will not deny the transcendent realm; but he is still a son of the black earth, and the world of pure forms is beyond his competence to experience directly. Here is Milosz's handling of contradiction in the *Treatise:*

> Yesterday a snake was darting across the road at dusk.
> Run over by a car, it writhed on the asphalt.
> But we are both the snake and the wheel. There are two
> Dimensions. Here is the truth
> Of unattainable essence, here, at the edge
> Of what lasts and what does not, two lines intersect.
> Time lifted above time by time.   (quoted in CCM, 181)

Read superficially this might seem as platonic as Weil's aesthetic. Only a few specific changes separate the two. Essence is unattainable—that is, the eternal cannot be perceived directly. Without time we are nothing, we require a temporal eternity.

In a later explication of this particular passage, Milosz had recourse to traditional theology (as paradoxical as this might seem). There have always been schools that sought to achieve the immutable. "But when it came to discussing an eternity utterly devoid of the flow of time, the theologians concluded that there still must be some sort of time in an eternity conceived as paradise, heaven; so they introduced the concept of *aevum* instead of *aeternum*, a time different from the earth's but still a variation on it, because man cannot imagine anything outside of time, nothing can exist without developing" (CCM, 181). This is what Milosz is seeking and what poetry at its best strives for: *aevum*. He must build his eternal values out of time. *Treatise on Poetry* is based on a dialectic of almost Hegelian proportions. We start life in nature with a time that is pure recurrence, the sequence of the seasons. Such life had been destroyed in places like Issa Valley. Yet in Milosz's mind, a natural life was still an option, at least for him. His friend Thornton Wilder recommended that, after his defection, he withdraw to an American farm. There he would be able to enjoy eternal recurrence and write pure poetry. He could also study the eternal languages of Hebrew and Greek.

But if such a life was still possible, Milosz could not accept it. This would cost him what he called the "granularity of historical time." He might be able to convince himself that he was contemplating eternal forms directly, with time and space only supplying occasions for the transcendence of his limitations. In the *Treatise* he speaks of this option wistfully:

> Silences, and dreams about the structure of the world, which
>   deserve
> respect. The eternal questions
> did not attract us as they should, nor did purity.
> Quite the reverse, every day we wanted
> to raise the dust of names and events with our voices

But why should he be preoccupied with the dust of history, the granularity of time? The simple answer is that, in reality, he had no choice. In a little-known essay written in 1957, he makes the point as follows:

> The centuries which separate us from the Middle Ages are not like a blackboard which can be easily sponged off leaving no trace of what had been written on it; we can no longer accept as our own the view of life of Dante, while at the same time launching artificial satellites into the ionosphere. That static image of the world is inaccessible to us; it was not known at that time that man is a historical being and is submitted to society to such an extent that the very air he breathes is conditioned by it.[8]

Here we have come to the second part of the dialectic, the antithesis expressed in *Treatise on Poetry* in the section "The Spirit of History." He insists that the older belief that "visible beauty / Is a little mirror for beauty of being" has simply collapsed before the spirit of history, which makes change the measure of all things:

> The golden house, the word *is,* collapses
> And the word *becomes* ascends to power.   (CP, 115)

Everything collapses before history and time. We worship "ungraspable Movement" and thereby deny our own existence:

> Now we are equal to the gods
> Knowing in you that we do not exist.   (CP, 116)

In good Hegelian fashion, the antithesis points to its own inadequacy. Both thesis and antithesis contain part of the truth and so now can be subsumed into a greater whole. Weil and those who wish to ascend to the world of platonic forms are right; we must seek the eternal. Those who would reduce everything to the flux of all that has been are also correct; we cannot escape time, even in our wildest dreams or within the holy of holies. So we must find the eternal within the temporal. This is done not in the propositions of philosophy, or even in the wordy prose of novels and essays, but in the weighted forms of poetry.

Milosz can summarize this dialectic in a single sentence: "First, time is only biological continuity; then comes historical time, connected with memory, and then—I don't know—contact with God, the acquiring of lasting, immutable values, but through a rootedness in time" (CCM, 182). We should note that the last stage is introduced with an aporia; this stage is not knowledge. As he puts it in the *Treatise:*

> From smashed armor, from eyes stricken
> By time's command, and returned
> To the jurisdiction of mold and fermentation,
> Comes our hope.   (182)

Or, as he asks in another poem of the fifties,

> Do you agree then
> To abolish what is, and take from movement
> The eternal moment as a gleam
> On the current of a black river?[9]

With the publication of *Treatise on Poetry* Milosz was ready once again to write lyrics.[10] His poems from the period immediately after its publication dominate his next collection, *King Popiel* (1962). Many of these show the playful exuberance of a poet who has experienced the full recovery of his creative powers. The themes of the new poems are much the same as those found in the *Treatise,* but the tone is very different.

There is, for example, "Magpiety." Here a magpie seen in a French forest reminds him of one he saw as a child in Lithuania, "the same but not quite the same," just as he is the same but not quite the same as the child he once was. He is amazed. Is there, he asks himself, such a thing as magpiety? Such a thing as an essential core, unchanging being in endless becoming? He can never comprehend such an essence, the quality of magpiety, but he must believe in it for the sake of his own being:

> If however magpiety does not exist
> My nature does not exist either.
> Who would have guessed that, centuries later,
> I would invent the question of universals?   (CP, 120)

The mock wonder of the last line directs readers to treat this serious subject as a form of philosophic playfulness. The playful tone carries into other poems. There is the comically absurd legend retold in "King Popiel," of a man eaten by mice and who yet, by the poet's sleight of hand, becomes the sinister inheritor of the scientific weltanschauung in which he can "smooth, on his throne, his javelin with a knife." Sometimes he draws the reader into the game. In "Heraclitus" he invites us to turn the great celebrator of flux on his head:

> Particular existence keeps us from the light.
> (That sentence can be read in reverse as well.)   (CP, 130)

The first assertion, a flat statement of the Greek rationalism that Simone Weil loved so well, argues that we must shed our individuality if we are to achieve the universal light. Reversed, the assertion reads: The light keeps us from particular existence.

This is Caliban's little joke on his dear Ariel. And even when the poem seems to fall back on a despair over poetry's final inability to save anything, the poet can slyly undercut his pessimism. In "No More" we are told that since "Out of reluctant matter / What can be gathered? Nothing, beauty at best," the poet has become an arranger of "verses about cherry blossoms, / Chrysanthemums and the full moon." But in the middle stanza of the poem he offers an extraordinarily vivid portrait of Venetian courtesans:

> If only I could describe the Courtesans of Venice
> As in a loggia they teased a peacock with a twig,
> And out of brocade, the pearls of their belt,
> Set free heavy breasts and the reddish weal
> Where the buttoned dress marked the belly,
> As vividly as seen by the skipper of galleons
> Who landed that morning with a cargo of gold.   (CP, 123)

Later he was to say of this passage that it "paradoxically shows us the poet achieving what, in his opinion, was beyond his power (WP, 73).[11]

Occasionally Milosz's play can go beyond what the poem can bear, at least for most readers. The original ending of "Milan" is the first line of a couplet from the great poet Mickiewicz: "Whoever has not touched earth." Readers were expected to supply the second line: "Will never be in heaven," but will also have to see that the couplet, set in "Milan," has changed meaning and requires a sort of Caliban-esque revision, such as: "Who has not touched the earth / has not touched heaven." Milosz came to see that this complicated game expected too much of readers and in *Collected Poems* drops the Mic-kiewicz line (though he retains it in the notes, along with a hint of its proper interpretation in the new setting).

Even when Milosz confronts the horrors of history in *King Popiel* he manages to do so with composure. His cycle "From the Chroni-cles of the Town of Pornic" (CP, 137–140) starts in Bluebeard's castle, moves through executions and rapine, but ends with "Our Lady of Recovery." We have learned from the flux of time that we are but children and humanity is a beloved family. And our Lady of Recov-ery stretches her hands and smiles: "Her smile meant that it was all according to her will."

Immediately after the publication of *Treatise on Poetry*, Milosz began a prose account of his recovery—or rather of his illness as well as his recovery. *Native Realm* was the title in its English translation, but the original is probably better rendered as "Native Europe." Here he does not celebrate his individuality but offers a detached account of how his Europe produced the author of the *Treatise*.

He subtitled the book: "A Search for Self-Definition."[12] This search is not intended to be ultimately successful. His definitions of himself will be a personal humiliation, for only through that process, through a purgatory, will he be able to approach what is sacred within himself, the divine promise. The failure of each succeeding self-definition will strip away another layer of historical necessity. His first self-definition is as a typical Central European of his own genera-tion. As such, Milosz is obsessed with the instability of human things, an obsession at the core of his earliest catastrophist poems and one he has never lost: "Man's fleetingness seen against a back-ground of unchanging nature affords an inexhaustible subject for meditation" (161). At times, however, the obsession is so intense that it becomes almost pathological:

> As far as I know, it does not figure in any psychiatric handbook. It consists of a disturbance in one's perception of time. The sick man constantly sees time as an hourglass through which states, systems, and civilizations trickle like sand; his immediate surroundings lose the force of reality; they do not last at all, they disintegrate; in other words, being is unreal, only movement is real. Those who plant flowers, till the fields, build houses are deserving of pity because they are seen as participants in a phantasmagoric spectacle, and to him they are no more real than to a demon who flies up to their windows at night and peeks through the pane. They are foredoomed because the order in which they have established themselves and which shapes their every thought and feeling is, like every order, ripe for destruction. (NR, 261–262)

Milosz is merciless in trying to account for everything about him-self in terms of external causes. The Lithuania of his childhood had numerous birds. Milosz has lived many places since, places he has judged good or bad. On reflection, he discovers that "good" usually means "the place has numerous birds." Most of what we know from our past has been learned unconsciously. "It is incredible how much of the aura of a country can penetrate to a child. Stronger than thought is an image—of dry leaves on a path, of twilight, of heavy sky" (45). The same is true of an adult. A mature man judges the place he is living to be good. He thinks he is judging it in terms of an ethical concept. On reflection, "good" turns out to be the image of a bird-laden tree. If this is so, if our vaunted concepts turn out upon analysis to be only faded sensory impressions, then should we not agree with Marxists that the individual is but the product of biolog-ical and historical forces over which he has no control?

This is the question to whcih Milosz quickly leads his reader. It is a question that Western Europeans might not be inclined to ask, once society returned to normal after the war. It is, however, a question that those from the other Europe cannot help asking again and again. Milosz is trying to make his readers share his obsession, to see this obsession as the beginning of wisdom.

How then does one resist the simple determinism, the simple scientism that would reduce man to a merely accidental collocation of atoms? Milosz, as he recollected it, began to struggle with the issue during his Catholic education. He had already then seen that his answer to reductionism had to be tied to a general solution of the problem of evil:

> If nature's law is murder, if the strong survive and the weak perish, and it has been this way for millions and millions of years, where is there room for God's goodness? Why must man, suspended on a tiny star in the void, no more significant than the microbes under a microscope, isolate his own suffering as though it were different from that of a bird with a wounded wing or a rabbit devoured by a fox . . . ? Such questions plunged me, sometimes for weeks, into a state bordering on physical illness. (77)

Milosz, to the displeasure of his teachers, found the most plausible response to the problem of evil in the Manichean heretics, who refused "to take refuge behind some vague will of God in order to justify cruelty. They called necessity, which rules everything that exists in time, the work of an evil Demiurge opposed to God. God, separated in this way from the temporal order, subsisted in a sphere proper to himself, free from responsibility, the object of our desires" (78).

Notice how his portrayal of his development before the 1930s parallels his development since. He first presents himself as the simple product of natural forces, much as he would have presented himself during his Wilno period. (The good is the image of a bird-laden tree.) He then discovers evil, a cruelty in nature so monstrous that his response cannot be one of mere assent—just as during his Warsaw period he becomes obsessed with the cruelty of history; the danger here is descent into nihilism. He finally finds a response to the problem in Manicheanism. He finds this Manicheanism not in Weil but in his church history textbooks. But when Milosz then presents us with a critique of the Manicheanism of his schoolboy days, we must also read it as a critique of Weilian metaphysics. The problem with Manicheanism, Milosz discovered, was in its ethics.

Manicheanism can produce ascetic saints like Weil, beings so pure that they scarcely seem human. But what of the Calibans who are firmly entrenched in this world of matter, those who take animal pleasure in satisfying their biological needs, who have to make their way in a corrupt and corrupting world? For such Calibans, Manicheanism is a dangerous world view because it provides a rationalization for inhuman behavior—"if we are in the power of Evil, we should sin out of spite, immerse ourselves in it as deeply as possible in order to despise ourselves the more" (78). We can slit someone's throat and weep sorrowful tears over the victim—and there will be no inconsistency in this. We intended brotherhood, but the world demands death and we are in the power of the world. We are not to blame, the evil of the world is. And we will lead the chorus in bitterly denouncing a world that has made us murder. Dangerous, then, is a Manicheanism that cuts off the intention from the act, the self from the world.

Milosz tells of an incident he witnessed in January 1945. He was in a large country house with about a dozen Soviet soldiers. Toward the center of a room, a man is standing who could not have been much over thirty. He wears a long white sheepskin coat and has the type of attractive face often seen in the Rhine country. The man is a German prisoner of war, a conquistador now conquered:

> Maybe I should have hated him, above all for the stupidity that, multiplied by the stupidity of millions like him, conferred power on Hitler and made of this young German the blind instrument of murder. But I found no hate in myself. I imagined him, for some reason, on a sunny slope, in a drill, pushing a wheelbarrow full of shoots from fruit trees. They did not hate him either. Because, like a caged animal, he was afraid of the unknown, one of them got up and gave him a cigarette; that movement of the hand meant reconciliation. Another clapped him on the back. Then an officer went up to him and slowly, distinctly, pronounced a long speech. It was useless because the Ger-

man understood nothing, but he glued his eyes to the speaker's lips like a dog who strains to guess the meaning of his master's words. Yet from the friendly tone he concluded that they did not want revenge, did not want to harm him. "Don't be afraid," the officer stressed repeatedly. "Nothing bad will happen to you, the war is already over, you are no longer an enemy but an ordinary man. You will work for peace and will be sent to the rear right away." The pity, even cordiality in the voice, the mild, grave tone of authority quieted the prisoner and he smiled timidly: gratitude. Though no command had been given, one of the soldiers sleepily picked himself up from his bench and took the prisoner from the room. The rest fell back into their previous apathy of physically exhausted human beings. In a few minutes the soldier returned alone, dragging a white sheepskin coat that he threw next to his duffel bag. He sat down and rolled a cigarette. The melancholy way he inhaled his smoke and spat on the floor expressed the thoughts of all of them in that room on the frailty of human life: "That's fate." (NR, 141–142)

The Russian soldiers hated this helpless German soldier no more than Milosz did. They killed him without malice and out of necessity—the difficulty of transferring him to the rear or perhaps their need for his sheepskin coat. Their soothing of him was more than simple hypocrisy. In fact, they had played out their little comedy more for themselves than for him; it was a "tribute to what should be, since they knew all the while that reality runs along quite opposite tracks" (143–144). Herein lies the great danger of Manicheanism.

This is not so much a rejection of the saintly Weil as a rejection of Weil's philosophy as part of this world. And so Milosz must develop his own theory that will place the divine within, not beyond, our experience—and prevent us from embracing a dualism that separates the intention from the deed. This is only because he himself tried to embrace such a dualism and found himself incapable of sustaining it. His finding of something beyond it helped him to emerge from what he called "My dark night of the soul, when I refused simply to slip out of the antinomy between the divine and the historical that was poisoning my life" (296). To explain how he emerged from this dark night, he provides a prose synopsis of *Treatise on Poetry*.

He has realized that he must use contradiction differently from Weil. He could not use it as a lever of transcendence, as a way of getting to the Holy Spirit. He must use it rather as a lever of immanence, a way of getting to the divine within things. This is Caliban's response to Ariel. Milosz will never deny the transcendent realm; but he is still a son of the black earth, and the world of forms is beyond his competence to experience directly.

This may be a limitation in Milosz, but it is a limitation that is essentially connected with his vocation as an artist. As Milosz writes so pointedly, "Artists crave being, a communion with the divine promise inside creation" (294). Weil might aspire to, believe she has achieved, communion with being outside the things of this world, but when she returns from the heights she will not find herself any better equipped to respond to the changing conditions of our existence, precisely because she will be inclined to deny temporality as a mere delusion. There is nothing but woe for "those who deceive themselves by their obedience to an unchanging moral claim, because for them historical time, which demands of us constant renewal, is but fog and delusion. Even their art will be inert for it has not been toughened in the purgatorial fires—and man's unavoidable contradictions are his purgatory" (295). The inertness of art is, of course, crucial for Milosz.

Weil the mystic contends that one can apprehend values directly, and we will thereby intuit their transcendence over any particular verbal formulation. Milosz the artist can only respond that he experiences the good indirectly, within actual individuals, and his formulations of the good always depend on the language he uses. This language may be mere fog and delusion when viewed from Weil's height; but for the poor poet, a mere Caliban, it is all he has. He must find the divine *within* the flux. He is the captive mind who has achieved only the beginning of wisdom; he will hit his head against the walls of his cell with only the hope of someday reaching a larger cell within this purgatorial prison house. And it is best for his art that, in this sense, he remain a captive mind.

4

A Magic Mountain

In Paris during the 1950s, Milosz worked out an effective response to the nihilism of Witkiewicz, thanks in large part to the influence of Simone Weil. But by the end of the decade he was recognizing fundamental limitations in her work, both as practical ethics and as aesthetics. He had begun to develop his own aesthetics but had yet to address the related issues in ethics and politics. He was destined to do so far from Paris, at the edge of San Francisco Bay.

In 1960, after a semester as visiting professor, Czeslaw Milosz accepted a permanent position at the University of California, Berkeley. Now he no longer had to earn his living by his pen—and he would be well removed from the Byzantine politics of Paris. One of the first essays he wrote in Berkeley was an expression of relief, "Brognart: A Story Told over a Drink."

In Paris he had become interested in Gilbert Brognart, a young Frenchman who was trapped in Poland by the outbreak of World War II, slipped over to the Soviet Union only to be arrested and imprisoned as a spy, and finally died still in prison in 1951. Milosz had long wanted to write about him, but could not while he was in Paris:

"Because what to me was an abyss, the vision of an abyss, to them was only a weapon in a political game played for reasons other than Brognart" (EE, 3). In Paris everything was judged in political terms, especially whatever came from the pen of a prominent defector like Milosz. He could not bring himself to write about Brognart in such circumstances because his audience would only "yawn and turn away from the bore or wink knowingly: another shrewd fellow, even a skillful one, increasing political assets."

In Berkeley Milosz could write about how a photograph of Brognart reminded him of a cousin who had died in a Nazi camp, about how Brognart "haunts me to this day, ever more closely merged with my cousin, so that I can barely tell them apart." He could write about all this not to make some ulterior political point, but as a form of praying, "Peace to their poor souls" (14).

This freedom from politics, however, was achieved only by accepting an exile that seemed, at least at first, to impose an almost aesthetic detachment from life: "No more running around, no more anticipating, no more being active, mixing, conversing—stranded in a zone of absolute alienation" (LU, 25). But even a professor of Slavic language and literature has to be active, to run around and converse. Milosz might have accepted the position simply as a means of livelihood, but he soon realized that it was going to be much more. It was going to be "a bridge spanning the earlier and the later passions" (29).

The earlier passion was Simone Weil; the later one he discovered through a professorial duty that came to him almost by chance. Since there was not enough student interest to have him teach Polish literature exclusively, he was assigned one of his department's most popular courses, Dostoevsky. In teaching this course he eventually found a new and powerful way to express his differences with Simone Weil; more immediately he found, as he began to teach the course, that he was faced with rhetorical problems not unlike Dostoevsky's own:

> Among my students very few think of themselves as Christians. The
> majority are indifferent toward Christianity, so that in teaching Dos-

toevsky I have always been aware of a paradox: for some, that course was a first encounter with matters of religion, yet nearly all shared something with those Russian intellectuals whose attitudes Dostoevsky abhorred.

So he "openly acknowledged the existence of good and evil, a stance they dismissed as irredeemably reactionary." Each year, then, irredeemably reactionary Professor Milosz would have to guide as many as one hundred California students through the major novels of Dostoevsky, and in the process would try to teach them something of Christianity and of their own responsibility, at least in part, for the good and evil in their lives.

Each year he would explain the moral intricacies of *Crime and Punishment*. He would explain to his students that Raskolnikov could kill the old woman only because he thought of her abstractly, as a pawnbroker and not as a person. He would explain that Raskolnikov was saved only because Sonya persisted in loving him, in responding to him not as a type, a criminal, but as a unique individual of infinite worth. Milosz would have to explain that Dostoevsky had not invented the theme of rebirth himself but had found it, during his prison years, in the New Testament writings attributed to the Apostle John. *Crime and Punishment* was a novelistic meditation on John's gospel, especially on the episode of the raising of Lazarus. Milosz told them the story of Lazarus: how Martha came out to meet Jesus after Lazarus died, how she got all the right answers to his questions (Jesus was the Son of God, the dead will rise again at the end of time, and so on) and yet he remained unmoved; then Mary came and she too got her catechism right, but she did something more, falling to the ground and weeping—then Jesus wept too. Abstract answers in John were not enough. Thomas asked Jesus for the knowledge that would enable the apostles to follow him when he went to God, but Jesus only replied, "I am the way, the truth, and the life"—literally, I am the true and living way. Thomas would be saved not by some abstract knowledge but by the touching of Jesus' wounds. The saving Word comes to Thomas in the flesh, much as the saving wisdom comes to Raskolnikov as Sonya. And just as abstraction enable Raskolnikov to kill the pawnbroker, so they enable the high priest to rationalize that "one man must die that a nation might live" and to plot the death of Christ. The deepening and clarification of Milosz's thought in *Visions from San Francisco Bay* can be partly attributed to his new distance from Europe, and partly to his careful and repeated reading of Dostoevsky.[1]

But if Milosz thought he would be removed from politics by being in Berkeley, the events of the 1960s proved him wrong. The very students to whom he was lecturing were also bringing the university to a standstill by demonstrating, sometimes violently, against the university administration and against Vietnam. Milosz found in Dostoevsky a text that helped him to understand what was going on around him in his adopted country, the very novel that his undergraduates found most disturbing to read, *The Devils*. And if reading it did not disturb them, his lectures on it surely did.

Dostoevsky, Milosz would explain, regarded the Enlightenment as a disease. Those eighteenth-century liberals might seem benign as they preached the brotherhood of man—liberty, fraternity, equality. But they were using the authority of science to argue that mankind can save itself through the acquisition of knowledge, through abstractions. Enlightenment would bring the heavenly city to earth, or so they thought. The terror of the French Revolution gave a glimpse of what such enlightenment could really bring to earth. But, in general, liberalism had not yet shown its demonic side in Western Europe. It was a disease, but people in Western Europe had developed partial immunities by having been exposed to it for so long. In Eastern Europe things would be different.

In a paper delivered at a Slavic studies conference, he made succinctly the point repeated over and over in his undergraduate lectures: "Educated Russians assimilated in a few decades ideas that had taken two or three centuries to mature in the West. As with those diseases that remain harmless for natives but become lethal when transplanted abroad, the dilemma—philosophy and science versus religion—acquired an exceptional virulence in Russin minds" (LU,

51). Among the Russian intelligentsia the disease ran its course almost immediately. The western Enlightenment made them like men possessed, insanely bent on their own destruction. Such a process of nihilistic self-destruction is what Dostoevsky dramatized in *The Devils*. And Milosz, when he lectured on this book, hinted that it was a mirror in which his students might find images of themselves. All this was made explicit in his meditations on his California experiences in *Visions*.

Much of the first half of that book Milosz devotes to his general philosophical vision, the vision we delineated in the first chapter. This part of the book culminates in his poem "To Robinson Jeffers." After that, Milosz focuses his attention on the California social scene as he observed it in the 1960s. Here is his account of the most famous student demonstration that disrupted the University of California during Milosz's first decade there:

> A few years ago in Berkeley, watching fourteen thousand students sitting on the stone benches of the Greek Theater reacting with one great hostile shout at the speech by the university's president, Clark Kerr (a liberal), I realized that, to understand any of this, one would have to measure it by another country, another century. The strength of the collective emotion was not in proportion to the causes of their dissatisfaction, trivial if viewed rationally . . . The students in the Greek Theater were united by the tacit and, for them, obvious premise that any authority issuing from an evil system and protecting that system was itself pure evil. Isn't this the nineteenth-century Russian intelligentsia? (VSF, 127)

Just as Dostoevsky used the nihilism of the Russian intelligentsia as an argument against western liberalism, so Milosz believed that the escapism of his American students was itself a reductio ad absurdum of postwar European thought.

He himself had seen at first hand the emptiness of postwar Paris. "The European spirit hated itself, turned against itself, and derided the institutions it had elaborated, perhaps thus masking a painful sense of its own disgrace." Culture then became "an orgy, a pandemonium of all the disgust," and was dominated by the "fashion-able discourses on *la nausée,* the absurd, alienation" (118–119).

Milosz ironically comments that, given such a self-destructive set of beliefs, "how Western Europe has functioned from the day the war ended until today, as I write, is a perfect mystery to me." But of course he knew very well how. That set of beliefs was only a convenient way to strike an impressive pose. (As he put it in his Brognart essay, "French rationalism is a legend, unless reducing everything to eloquence is taken for rationalism"; EE, 12.) Intellectuals vied with one another to convey to the masses this "mood of impotence, linked with sullen buffoonery"; but while Western Europe's mind was devoting itself to venomous laughter, its body was "eating, drinking, and buying automobiles and refrigerators (by the grace of America)" (118–119). It lived, much as the Enlightenment had earlier, on its own hypocrisy.

The French might not take their fashionable nihilism seriously, but these American students, much like the Russian intelligentsia of the nineteenth century, were taking it very seriously indeed. The result was "the erosion of the system of ideas and customs which form the American way of life" (133). Milosz remembers once visiting Sacra-mento, the state capital but an otherwise undistinguished city, the kind of place he certainly would never want to live:

> It was there that a student, a young simpleton, asked me how life in Sacramento differed from life in a concentration camp. I had to assure him gently that there was a great difference, gently because even any persuasion would be lost on a person unable to distinguish between a pinprick and the rack. This young idiot had never faced starvation, he took a bath every day, drove a car, an old one but his own; he could take the works of Lenin and Mao Tse-tung from the library, and so he had forgotten what has first place in the hierarchy of human needs. (146–147)

Milosz responds to small-town American life much as Dostoevsky did to the peasant life of his Russia. He regards it as the foundation of the country and the source of its strength. He describes in loving detail a parade he once saw in Myrtle Point, Oregon—the floats, the various local beauty queens ("Much regal beauty—the queens of the melon growers, of the fishermen, of the country, the town. They throw kisses, smiles"), the drill teams, the 4-H contests. All that his students would regard with repugnance or embarrassment he applauds:

> The difference between us is that, for me, all the frameworks that permit the daily practice of virtue are very fragile, it is easy to destroy them, as I saw for myself while observing ideologically planned regimes at close range. Virtue: to be thirteen years old, jump up every day at dawn to feed, water, and brush your own horse, bullock, ram, to learn everything that could ensure victory in the livestock competition. The long-haired revolutionary, usually raised in a big city in a well-to-do family, has no idea that a few thoughtless edicts are enough to ruin agriculture and set the lives of farm children on a completely different course, not necessarily a better one. (158)

Looking at American farming communities, Milosz saw other Issa valleys waiting for destruction at the hands of new commissars. Looking at his students he found some who would aspire to be such commissars.

California, therefore, did not provide Milosz with an escape from the dark politics of Europe. In fact he found there forces of darkness at work with frightening effectiveness. Earlier he had thought that Witkiewicz's prophecy of the pill of Murti-Bing was being figuratively fulfilled by communist ideology. But in California he found it being literally fulfilled in the drug culture. LSD, its apostles assured, would bring the Age of Aquarius, a placidity and indifference they called wisdom. Even Aldous Huxley claimed that LSD would open the doors of perception so that we might experience a chemically induced conversion to eastern philosophy. Murti-Bing, indeed.

What was western philosophy doing against this onslaught? Milosz found that the most influential philosopher-professor at the University of California was the heterodox Marxist, Herbert Marcuse. For Milosz, Marcuse's writings exuded a frightening "hatred for man as he is in the name of man as he ought to be" (191). (This hatred Milosz found confirmed in the one conversation he had with Marcuse.) The young found Marcuse attractive, Milosz thought, because he provided them with an excuse; they could blame society as the source of all that ailed them. Dostoevsky "noted a similar tendency among the Russian intelligentsia, who did not recognize individual guilt, holding the environment responsible instead" (189). The American students, under all their high moral causes, were infected with the same self-destructive drives that Dostoevsky portrayed in *The Devils:*

> Their "let it be" means "let the destruction be" . . . As with the Russian nihilists, their desire for a general conflagration is the final link in a self-begetting chain. They also recall the Russian nihilists by the way they exclude themselves from the mass of their own people, whom they view as benighted, and thus a burden. (193)

In a poem of the late sixties Milosz indirectly addressed the nihilistic rage that he saw in so many American youth. He told the story of Meader, a mountain man who was pestered by a grizzly bear. No normal grizzly, this one had become so bold and malicious that he ignored men and was not afraid of fire. When the grizzly finally began to attack the cabin, Meader shot him. He followed the trail of the mortally wounded bear until he came across the corpse. Examining it, he understood what lay behind the bear's behavior:

> Half of the beast's jaw was eaten away by an abcess, and caries.
> Toothache, for years. An ache without comprehensible reason,
> Which often drives us to senseless action
> And gives us blind courage. We have nothing to lose,
> We come out of the forest, and not always with the hope
> That we will be cured by some dentist from heaven.   (CP, 233)

When *Visions from San Francisco Bay* was first published in 1969, Milosz could not have expected that it would be translated into English—French perhaps, but not English. To read the book is at times like eavesdropping on a conversation among Europeans, a conversation in which one of them is trying to explain to the rest the lotus land called California. Nonetheless, by the time *Visions* was published, Milosz had already started preparing a volume of his poems for an American publisher. What role could he have envisioned for himself within the increasingly nihilistic American culture he had described so unsparingly in *Visions?* Two of the essays are revealing in this regard. The first has to do with a locally well-known Berkeley eccentric called Holy Hubert:

> For several years this small, freckled man has stood every day at his post by the entrance to the university campus in Berkeley. He is an evangelist, a preacher of the teachings of Jesus. I have practically never seen him speak calmly. He is usually thrashing about in something like a trance, redfaced, with swollen veins and drops of sweat on his dandruff-covered forehead; his noisy exhortations and thunderings against sin do not carry very far because hoarseness makes his voice break in a choked falsetto. His is such a part of the colorful carnival atmosphere that practically no one stops for him, never more than four or five listeners, who regard him with mellow smiles and sometimes amuse themselves by asking him questions if his enthusiasm slackens and he has to be reexcited. He is a popular figure, a part of the local folklore like the boys in their saffron robes chanting "Rama Krishna, Krishna Rama" over and over, and the students treat him with the benevolence one shows the harmlessly insane. (132)

But Milosz refuses to treat Holy Hubert as insane: he is just out of place. He would be treated with perfect seriousness in the small towns of Arkansas or Kentucky, but here, on the west coast, history has passed him by—and he has failed to adapt. "Perhaps he wishes to imitate St. Paul preaching in pagan Athens, but he is completely unaware of any of the historical changes occurring now" (133).

The unsuccessful "Evangelical Emissary" (as Milosz calls him) is in marked contrast to the subject of the next essay: Henry Miller, an evangelical whose time had come in the California sixties. Milosz knew Miller briefly in Paris, before he became the honored prophet of the sexual revolution (with *Playboy* magazine, for instance, making him the subject of a lavishly illustrated article). In Paris, Milosz had thought him an interesting writer.[2] "Miller's volcanic roar, indifferent to all authority, is fascinating, exciting, and . . . he is sometimes dazzling in the freshness of his judgments" (140). Milosz recognizes that Miller's roar had become profoundly influential in American literature; for instance, Allen Ginsberg's "hysterical howl comes primarily from Miller." Henry Miller had found his audience, leaving Milosz to regret the "immature confusion of his mind."

Milosz thought of Miller as an American, plebian version of that proud Lucifer of European nihilism, Friedrich Nietzsche: "Something disturbing occurs when Americans throw themselves on European authors, especially Nietzsche. The play of their contradictions disappears, a certain trait of humor hidden beneath their fury, which only the historical imagination provides, whereas what the Americans extract are the elements which allow them reconciliation with the ideal of the 'natural man' " (139). Milosz no doubt had more in his mind than Nietzsche and Miller when he wrote those words. He too was a European author who liked the play of contradiction and whose fury is frequently mitigated by historically grounded humor. He must have questioned how well his voice would be heard, or at least understood, in a world dominated by Miller's roar and Ginsberg's howl. Moreover, if he spoke too plainly he was likely to be dismissed as a buffoon, much as Holy Hubert unwittingly played the clown in the many-ringed circus that was Berkeley.

At the end of his essay on Hubert, Milosz wrote: "At least, thanks to him, I can puzzle out how the two systems of ideas and customs, the old and the new, relate to each other. If it were up to me, I would prefer not to be forced to choose between them" (135). But he knew that he was going to have to choose between them. If not between Holy Hubert and Henry Miller, then between Dostoevsky and Sartre, or between the virtuous life at Myrtle Point and the self-destructive ideas of the New Left. And he knew that choosing involved a complicated, if not distorting, transaction with an American audience given to reductionist readings of European authors—and given to expecting in their own authors shrillness of assent or dissent, humorless choices without qualification, with no historical imagination to foresee where reduction led.

This was the very audience for which, in 1971, he was preparing his first book of poems in English. How to bridge the gap between *his* choice and what they would reduce it to? He indirectly addresses the problem in one essay of the period, written with a bitterness that perhaps measures his own sense of the futility of the project:

> One thing is absolutely incomprehensible to me in all the success of such Russian writers as Pasternak or Solzhenitsyn with the Western public, especially Western literary critics . . . Any normal human being who reads these Russian writers in America, for instance, must have one dominant feeling—that of shame. Not because he himself is privileged, lives in an affluent society, and is not endangered by the whims of those in power, while the Russian writers tell of suffering imposed upon millions of their fellowmen, but because freedom of choice is being misused today by Western writers for the purpose of creating dehumanized literature perhaps, it is true, under the pretext of rebelling against a dehumanized world. But are the Western writers themselves conscious of the difference between genuine concern and what is just subservience to fashion or a marketing device? (EE, 79–80)

Fashionable in the west are "literary stripteases" and the "crazy, careening rush of artistic revolutions succeeding each other" (84). As a writer, Milosz confesses that he has considerable esteem for the technical virtuosity of these revolutionaries. As a writer he can esteem, but as a human being he is saddened.

He then turns to the examples of Pasternak and Solzhenitsyn. To be sure, Pasternak's poetics are silly and Solzhenitsyn's narrative at times creaks with the influence of socialist realism. Still their works " 'judge' all contemporary literature by reintroducing a hierarchy of values, the renunciation of which threatens mankind with madness." What infuriates Milosz is that critics and readers do not recognize the necessity of choosing between these two strands in contemporary literature, the morally hierarchical and the aesthetically self-destructive. "And how can literary critics writing on Pasternak or Solzhenitsyn so easily shirk their duty, which calls them to point out this ominous disparity?" (84).

Selected Poems is in its own way an attempt to reintroduce a hierarchy of values into the cultural world of roar and howl. The crucial word here is hierarchy. There are certainly significant questions in Miller and Ginsberg—Miller says yes to Eros and Ginsberg says no to America. Certainly their literary stripteases provide ample opportunity for displays of verbal virtuosity. But they leave the reader without a hierarchy of values, without the qualifications or sense of proportion that can be conveyed by the play of contradictions, by humor historically grounded. Without such hierarchy, we will end in a shrieking destructiveness, itself a symptom of madness. There are higher values than Myrtle Point, but they will not destroy Myrtle Point as the price of their being implemented. This is what he wished to teach.

The first poem of *Selected Poems,* "The Task," is emblematic of how Milosz will attempt to reintroduce this hierarchy, to teach moderation in the play of contradiction. It seems to have been written specifically to introduce the volume (and would appear in a Polish collection only in 1974).[3]

> In fear and trembling, I think I would fulfill my life
> Only if I brought myself to make a public confession
> Revealing a sham, my own and of my epoch:
> We were permitted to shriek in the tongue of dwarfs and
>   demons
> But pure and generous words were forbidden
> Under so stiff a penalty that whoever dared to pronounced one
> Considered himself a lost man.   (SP, 15; CP, 231)

Milosz conceded much here to the howlers against the epoch, and the shriekers against themselves. At least he concedes their powers of seduction. They seem to offer a way of fulfilling a life otherwise doomed to silent despair. Together, they offer the relief of confession and the satisfaction of having done one's duty (and perhaps considerably more than satisfaction). But at what cost? Above all, the cost of a truly human voice and of good words. For in the world of Miller and Ginsberg, confession and prophecy, miraculously, have been reduced to one thing: a shriek of a dwarf and demon. To yield to that shriek is to surrender most of one's humanity. Thus the necessity of balancing shrieks with other tones. To concede all to the shriek is to abandon the ability to *contain* shrieks in a hierarchical structure (such as a poem) that would judge shrieks for what they are. So Milosz seems to refuse the temptation but does not, at the same time, give his readers any "pure and general words" to counter it. What then is the "task" and has it been performed?

It is a proclamation of Milosz's intention for this book, but a proclamation that may be in the subjunctive mood. (The subjunctive plays no important role in Ginsberg or Miller.) This task, although in one sense not performed, is, in another, performed in the very saying, albeit in a qualified way. The poet's fury—at his age, at himself—is expressed, yet muffled, as if something prevented him from full expression. What a true experience of evil does (and evil was something Milosz knew better than Ginsberg or Miller) is to leave one not just with the temptation to scream negation but also with the recognition that even affirmations, if too pure, render one "a lost man."

The next poem—"Should, Should Not"—is an ironic celebration of the acceptance of limitations:

> A man should not love the moon.
> An axe should not lose weight in his hand.
> His garden should smell of rotting apples
> And grow a fair amount of nettles.
> A man when he talks should not use words that are dear to
>   him,
> Or split open a seed to find out what is inside it.
> He should not drop a crumb of bread, or spit in the fire
> (So at least I was taught in Lithuania).
> When he steps on marble stairs,
> He may try, the boor, to chip them with his boot
> As a reminder that the stairs will not last forever.   (16)

We are to realize that life is a play of contraries—shoulds and should nots. These constitute commandments humans ought to live by. Of course these commandments will not be offered in a schematic form wholly inapplicable to a world in which contraries themselves are never neatly symmetrical. The first "should nots" pose a pair of oppositions—aspiration to romance or purity as against the need for rootedness in the earth—but pose them in such a way that the balance is all in favor of the second part of the pair. Thus rootedness in the rich earth also involves labor (such as chopping wood), spoilage (such as rotten apples), and pain (such as the sting of nettles)— each of these is a limitation on human aspiration beyond earth. The next "should nots" deal with the sin of impiety, against carelessness with language and against life's sacred origin. These lead to imperatives derived from folk wisdom (learned by the poet in his homeland), which has a practical side: against waste of what satisfies hunger and against abuse of the precious element of fire. The final commandment is not put in the form of a should/should not, but is offered as a description of an act of boorishness; the boor here is our nature reminding us of the transience of the most solid-seeming graces of civilization, another assertion of limitation. Milosz himself has called the poem a "defense of the middle road" (CCM, 204). This is the road that takes us through the country of our native realm as a reminder of what we should (or should not) hope for. The tongue-in-cheek acceptance of superstition here doesn't subvert the seriousness of the call to acknowledge limits.

In the third poem, "Lessons," Milosz tries to show his readers that they should not (as Marcuse would have them) blame their faults on the society in which they were brought up. He himself was brought up in land close to the pastoral ideal, and the people there treated him with tenderness:

> From them I received the names of plants and birds,
> I lived in their country that was not too barren,
> Not too cultivated, with a field, a meadow
> And water in a boat moored behind a shed. (17)

Yet he finds within himself an inexplicable propensity for evil:

> This humiliated me.
> So that I wanted to shout: you are to blame
> For my not being what I want and being what I am.

And in this desire to make others responsible for the perversity and wickedness, he ultimately has to invoke the Garden of Eden:

> Sunlight would fall in my book upon Original Sin.
> And more than once, when noon was humming in the grass
> I would imagine the two of them, with my guilt,
> Trampling a wasp beneath the apple tree in Eden.

It is, however, still "my guilt."

So *Selected Poems* continues. Poem after poem in the first section is concerned with the acceptance of limitations. Some explore the inherent limitations of language itself, its inability to grasp and hold reality. Others are based on the contrast between the perceptions of youth and those of maturity—in a few it is hard not to imagine an old poet trying to convey wisdom to a young audience. About half were written after Milosz came to Berkeley; the other poems are mostly from the exhuberant *King Popiel,* though he also includes a few earlier ones. For instance, there is "Mittelbergheim," his poetic convalescence, since the patience required by convalescence is its own kind of moderation.[4]

Still this tepid wisdom of the first section has its own danger. The individual—here, the poet—can come to such a strong sense of his own limitations that he succumbs to them; he can come to think of his own individuality as a mere nothing, a flaw to be overcome. This danger Milosz began to explore in the last few poems of the section—most notably "To Raja Rao," a poem originally written in English as a response to a fellow writer who exhorted Milosz to study eastern philosophy and religion as a cure for his preoccupation with the self (SP, 29–31; CP, 226–228). He begins the poem by tracing his own development from a youthful visionary to a maturity in which

limitations are accepted, as well as his own responsibility for his
failings:

> Raja, I wish I knew
> the cause of that malady.

> For years I could not accept
> the place I was in.
> I felt I should be somewhere else.

> A city, trees, human voices
> lacked the quality of presence.
> I would live by the hope of moving on.

> Somewhere else there was a city of real presence,
> of real trees and voices and friendship and love . . .

> I learned at last to say: this is my home,
> here, before the glowing coal of ocean sunsets,
> on the shore which faces the shores of your Asia,
> in a great republic, moderately corrupt.

He admits, nonetheless, that his acceptance of his situation has not
brought him peace of mind. Now that he no longer blames the
societies in which he has lived for his faults, he finds his consciousness
turning against itself:

> Raja, this did not cure me
> of my guilt and shame.
> A shame of failing to be
> what I should have been . . .

> Tormented by my ego, deluded by it
> I give you, as you see, a ready argument.

He gives him a ready argument because Raja advocates an overcoming of the ego, a dissolving of the individual self into the Absolute.
Milosz will even concede to Raja that this eastern solution to his
problem is not really alien to the western tradition; he will concede
that "Socratic wisdom is identical with your guru's." Milosz will then
simply reject both Greek rationalism and eastern religion:

No, Raja, I must start from what I am.
I am those monsters which visit my dreams
and reveal to me my hidden essence.

He will persist in asserting his individuality as fundamental:

Greece had to lose, her pure consciousness
had to make our agony only more acute.

We needed God loving us in our weakness
and not in the glory of beatitude.

No help, Raja, my part is agony,
struggle, abjection, self-love and self-hate,
prayer for the Kingdom
and reading Pascal.

The assertion of self is emphatic, but made out of contradiction and
agony. Here Milosz is pointing beyond not just the philosophy of his
friend Raja and the nihilism of his own students, but also beyond the
unyielding rationalistic spirituality of Simone Weil. But what exactly
does Milosz see beyond it?

A reader of the first section of *Selected Poems* has perhaps been
weaned away from thinking that the pain of life has some simple
cure. The unbridled rage of Meader's grizzly will not do, nor will the
hope for some heavenly dentist. Milosz instead asks us to embrace
the agony itself. Yet the concluding poems of this section leave the
reader hanging. What is entailed by the persistent assertion of the
individual against the overpowering flow of time? What is the kingdom for which we are to pray while reading Pascal?

These are questions that are not immediately answered. First Milosz gives his readers a sense of how the flow of time has influenced
his own development as a poet. The untitled initial section of poems
is followed by "How once he was," three poems from his Lithuanian
period in which his readers see him as a son of the black earth singing
a hymn to that very earth to which he will return "as if my life had not
been." This section is followed by "What did he learn," in which the
reader can see how this pantheism was shattered by his experiences

during the war: "What is poetry which does not save / Nations or people?" Then the reader is ready to return to the questions rasied by "To Raja Rao." The final section suggests through its title some kind of resolution: "The Shore."

But what exactly is to be found across the all-threatening abyss of time? Is there perhaps a safer harbor of sorts for the beleaguered individual? And, if there is, how is it different from the immortality of Greek rationalism, a rationalism Milosz has already repudiated? Milosz's answers to these questions are so unconventional that they are best approached initially by way of his prose.

While *Selected Poems* was being published, Milosz was writing a pair of essays that explored the metaphysical, as opposed to the political, dimension of Dostoevsky's work. These essays provide a key to understanding the last section of *Selected Poems*. "Shestov or the Purity of Despair," published in 1973, centers on the early twentieth-century Russian thinker who tried to explain the philosophical insights of Dostoevsky. Lev Shestov believed that the key to Dostoevsky's work was the opposition between the individual and the idea, the particular and the universal. Life for Shestov is a continual struggle against losing a sense of one's uniqueness—just what Milosz had seen as the chief danger of his own wisdom in the first section of *Selected Poems*. Shestov saw this danger as inherent in any philosophy true to the ancient Greeks, for such philosophy always teaches the universal as the highest good: only the necessary, the general, and the eternally valid will merit investigation and reflection. This is why for Shestov the only fruit on the tree of knowledge is death. Knowledge entails the absorption of the individual by the universal, and even an ethics that prescribes universal norms for human behavior must be rejected. Thus "Saint Augustine hated the Stoics as much as Dostoevsky hated the liberals; both the Stoics and liberals recommended a morality of self-sufficing Reason" (EE, 107).

Not surprisingly, the thinker with whom Milosz believes Shestov can be most usefully compared is Simone Weil. Contemporaries (although unknown to one another), equally single-minded, both seeing the last three thousand years as one short moment, they also had the same "central theme of their thought, the phenomenon of suffering and death" (114). This common ground, however, only served to emphasize the fundamental disagreement between the two thinkers. Both Shestov and Weil regarded human beings as of inestimable worth, but Shestov valued them as individuals whereas Weil valued them for their capacity to be rationally impersonal. Weil wished us to renounce our individuality: "My existence diminishes God's glory. God gave it to me so that I may wish to lose it."

For Shestov this reasoning would epitomize the death that knowledge brings. This is the abyss into which Greek philosophy, all philosophy, leads us. The God of the Hebrews (a person) was not the God of the Greeks (an idea). To Shestov peace of mind itself was suspect. Milosz wrote, "He loved only those who, like Pascal . . . 'seek while moaning'" (105). Milosz portrayed himself in just these terms at the end of "To Raja Rao": "My part is agony . . . prayer for the Kingdom / and reading Pascal." And Milosz in this essay as well as in the poem sides with Shestov and Dostoevsky. He concedes that Socrates and Hindus teach the same thing (as Weil herself believed). He asserts the "great difference between our looking at ourselves as ciphers on a statistical sheet and our grasping our destiny as something that is personal and unique" (118).

Milosz first learned of Shestov in a Paris student hotel from a young Romanian dying of cancer, Sorana Gurian.

> To Sorana the God of the Scriptures defended by the stern priest Shestov would probably not have meant an afterlife and a palm tree in Heaven. He must have appeared to her as He did to the Russian author, as pure anti-Necessity. The question was not the existence of Heaven and Hell, not even the "existence" of God himself. Above any notions, but revealed by His voice in the Scriptures, He is able to create anything, even a personal heaven and earth for Sorana Gurian. Or for each one of us. (119)

Thus Milosz's essay ends, with the strange notion of a unique heaven and hell for each of us. But this is Milosz speaking, not Shestov. An infinite number of heavens and hells is to be found nowhere in

Shestov. Milosz in his essay implies that he found a fundamental limitation in Shestov. This defender of the individual, the particular, the personal, was in fact by talent as much a Greek as Weil. His tragedy was "that of lacking the talent to become a poet, and to approach the mystery of existence more directly than through mere concepts" (102).

Milosz had the talent Shestov lacked. More than that, he understood one key to Dostoevsky's art that Shestov had missed because he himself was not an artist. This was the foundation of Dostoevsky's art in the visions of Emanuel Swedenborg. And so Milosz's essay on Shestov is paired with one entitled "Dostoevsky and Swedenborg."

Swedenborg, a distinguished scientist of the early eighteenth century, had set himself an extraordinary task: "to demonstrate to the senses themselves the immortality of the soul." Swedenborg's own empirical examination of human anatomy and physiology, especially the brain, did not suffice for this. But in the 1740s visionary powers came to him. He was transported to "the other shore" (a phrase Milosz uses in this connection) and could see at first hand the endurance of human individuals beyond the grave. All individuality is preserved on this shore, both the good and the bad—hence there is an infinite variety, of both good and evil. Milosz quotes Swedenborg:

> Every evil, as well as every good, is of infinite variety. That this is a truth is beyond the comprehension of those who have only a simple idea regarding every evil, such as contempt, enmity, hatred, revenge, deceit, and other like evils. But let them know that each one of these evils contains so many specific differences, and each of these again so many instances of particular differences, that a volume would not suffice to enumerate them . . . Evidently, then, the hells are innumerable. (129–130)

The hell of Svidrigailov in *Crime and Punishment,* Milosz suggests, is a good example of a Swedenborgian hell. When Raskolnikov announces that he does not believe in a future life, Svidrigailov counters by asking what if there were only spiders there: "We always imagine eternity as something beyond our conception, something vast, vast! But why must it be vast? Instead of all that, what if it's one little room, like a bathhouse in the country, black and grimy and spiders in every corner, and that's all eternity is?" (quoted, 130).

The other shore, the immortality that Swedenborg wished to demonstrate to his senses, is not an overcoming of this world's particularity (as Weil or Plato would have it), but rather it is an experiencing of this particularity to the fullest. As Milosz puts it, "Every heaven or hell is a precise reproduction of the states of mind of a given man experienced when on earth and it appears accordingly—as beautiful gardens, groves, or the slums of a big city. Thus everything on earth perceived by the five senses will accompany a man as a source of joy or of suffering much as the alphabet, once learned, may be composed into comforting or depressing books" (127).

Will everything then be eternal? Will everything have immortality? Everything that has become an expressive part of a human consciousness. Any particular that is fully imagined, fully remembered by, say, a poet, will thereby be redeemed from time. Swedenborg "humanized or *hominized* God and the universe to such an extent that everything, from the smallest particle of matter to planets and stars, was given but one goal: to serve as a fount of signs for human language. Man's imagination, expressing itself through language and identical in its highest attainments with the Holy Ghost, was now to rule over and redeem all things by bringing about the era of the New Jerusalem" (140). This is the enterprise of the poems that Milosz placed as the last section of *Selected Poems,* "Shore." It would be tempting to try to divide the poems of "Shore" between those merely Shestovian and those fully Swedenborgian. Many of them, such as the powerful "To Robinson Jeffers," seek only the purity of Shestov's despair.

Occasionally, as in "A Gift," Milosz seems free of despair altogether, but on closer examination this proves illusory:

A day so happy.
Fog lifted early, I worked in the garden.

> Hummingbirds were stopping over honeysuckle flowers.
> There was no thing on earth I wanted to possess.
> I knew no one worth my envying him.
> Whatever evil I had suffered, I forgot.
> To think that once I was the same man did not embarrass me.
> In my body I felt no pain.
> When straightening up, I saw the blue sea and sails.   (118)

What distinguishes this experience from the mere childlike wonder—of, say, "The World"—is that even within the experience there is a sense of how ephemeral and exceptional are such moments. This of course is conveyed by the title. It is also conveyed by the unspoken contrasts that dominate the middle of the poem. He wanted to possess nothing (but he usually has wants). He envied no one (but he usually did envy). He forgot the evils he had suffered (evils he usually remembered). He was not embarrassed by himself (as he usually was). He felt no pain (but he usually did).

Such moments can strengthen one to face the impersonal demons that lurk beneath one's very feet. One must assert, moreover, that these demons will not triumph, that the individual is the real and will somehow survive against elemental powers:

> And what if Pascal had not been saved
> and if those narrow hands in which we laid a cross
> are just he, entire, like a lifeless swallow
> in the dust, under the buzz of the poisonous-blue flies?
>
> And if they all, kneeling with poised palms,
> millions, billions of them, ended together with their illusion?
> I shall never agree. I will give them the crown.
> The human mind is splendid; lips powerful,
> and the summons so great it must open Paradise.   (SP, 84;
>   CP, 150–151)

Milosz, however, wants immortality for more than just human beings. In one poem he asks, "What beautiful work / Will redeem the heartbeats of a living creature . . . ?" (SP, 114). This redemption for all particulars—not just the preference for them, as Shestov would have it, but the redemption—can be achieved only in a Sweden-borgian universe. So in one poem, "On the Other Side," where Milosz tries to imagine the death and subsequent experience of a damned soul, he begins with an epigraph from Swedenborg's *Heaven and Hell:*

> Some hells present an appearance like the ruins of houses
> and cities after conflagrations, in which infernal spirits dwell
> and hide themselves. In the milder hells there is an
> appearance of rude huts, in some cases contiguous in the form
>   of
> a city with lanes and streets.   (CP, 189)

Encouraged by the example of Swedenborg, Milosz tries repeatedly to reach out through his imagination and touch a reality otherwise lost, a reality that was the ground of his being, of all human being—the past. To save the past is not merely an honorable duty, but a way also of assuring his own present and future. For the imaginative recovery of the past, he now recognizes, is the only human way of giving immortality to time-bound mortals. Thus memory fused with imagination can bring back from the grave the most humble:

> Paulina, her room behind the servants' quarters, with one
>   window on the orchard
> where I gather the best apples near the pigsty
> squishing with my big toe the warm muck of the dunghill,
> and the other window on the well (I love to drop the bucket
>   down
> and scare its inhabitants, the green frogs).

Paulina is remembered, and then Milosz asserts:

> Paulina died long ago, but is.
> And, I am somehow convinced, not just in my consciousness.
>   (CP, 151–152)

The change in Milosz's understanding of his own work is shown dramatically in one poem of this last section. "Elegy for N.N."

was occasioned by a letter from Poland which informed him that a woman he once loved had recently died (CP, 239). He addresses her, wondering how she might have come to him, now that he is in California. But human memory is faulty and imagination not always at hand to do one's bidding. He tries to imagine her taxing journey across huge tracts of water and land, through cities and wilderness, until "then just a eucalyptus grove and you had found me." But he then apparently reverses himself and concludes negatively:

> No, it was not because it was too far
> you failed to visit me that day or night.
> From year to year it grows in us until it takes hold,
> I understood it as you did: indifference.

Here is the purity of despair, the individual feeling ultimately help-less in the face of inhuman might, this feeling itself disguised as indifference, detachment, distance. When Milosz wrote this poem, he understood it entirely in such negative terms; he thought himself to be only "emphasizing the distance separating me from the places of my childhood." But now, thanks to Swedenborg, he finds a deeper wisdom in the poem, more than he was aware of as he was writing it: "For N.N. visited me after all. And by writing about her, I proved that I was not indifferent."

This sense of her really having visited him and of himself having proven he was not indifferent—this did not entirely obliterate the despair. The mood of these later poems he calls in one of them "ecstatic despair." Milosz wishes to combine somehow the visionary ecstasy of Swedenborg with the purity of Shestov's despair. Most frequently he achieves this by juxtaposing the ecstasy of reliving some unique moment of experience with the despair of ever getting that moment into poetry.

The fully ecstatic despair is the theme of "Trumpets and Zithers," the cycle that concludes *Selected Poems*. The sequence is epitomized in its first line, "The gift was never named." Life is celebrated as an ecstatic gift, but the poet despairs of adequately naming it. In one poem the poet with "laughter and weeping" wonders how his consciousness can ever catch up with him "when I do not remember who I am":

> On many shores at once I am lying cheek on the sand and the
> same ocean runs in, beating its ecstatic drums.

In another poem he tries to capture in language what he once loved, but all he ends up with is a "grammatical form" and a "brocade of the style." Again and again he celebrates the present moment:

> In the hour of ending night it amazes—this place, this time,
> assigned for an awakening of this particular body.

Again and again he proclaims the inadequacy of language to capture the experience once it has passed: "My dishonest memory did not preserve anything, save the triumph of nameless births." Milosz has described this poem as a revolt against Greek philosophy: "I want to record something that exists and persists because it is individual, unique" (CCM, 226). Or as he puts it in "Trumpets and Zithers": "I wanted to describe this, not that, basket of vegetables / with a redheaded doll of a leek laid across it." Again: "Not ships but one ship with a blue patch at the corner of its sail."

The Greek will insist that only what is subsumed into the whole endures, but Milosz rebels: "What separates, falls. Yet my scream 'no!' is still heard / though it burned out in the wind. / Only what separates does not fall. All the rest is beyond / persistance." But his scream is burned out in the wind. His poetry, his cry, cannot save the individual. What can assure its persistance is a vision in which all, both past and present, are there at once, a vision both incomprehensible and dazzling.

The final poem of the cycle begins with an assertion of intense visionary ecstasy; it subordinates his individuality to something far greater, the energy of life itself, the surge of vitality that gives value to the individual, at the same time threatening individuality:

> A coelentera, all pulsating flesh, animal-flower,
> All fire, made up of falling bodies joined together by the black
> pin of sex.

> It breathes in the center of a galaxy, drawing to itself a star after
>   a star.
> And I, an instant of its duration, on multi-laned roads which
>   penetrate half-opened mountains.

But it ends with an admission of failure that is also an expression of faith in the future:

> I wanted to be a judge but those whom I called "they" have
>   changed into myself.
> I was getting rid of my faith so as not to be better than men
>   and
> women who are certain only of their unknowing.
> And on the roads of my terrestrial homeland turning round
>   with the music of the spheres
> I thought that all I could do would be done better one day.
>   (SP, 128)

Milosz's problem is that he has not been transported to the other shore as Swedenborg claimed to have been, any more than he had been captured by Christ as Weil had been. Swedenborg's shore is preferable to Weil's capture because it preserves the particularity of people and things. This seemed especially important in the light of Milosz's reading of Dostoevsky (with Shestov). A civilization that loses its sense of the uniqueness of individuals is a civilization doomed to barbaric self-destruction. Milosz found this confirmed not only in the nihilism among the students at Berkeley. The irredeemably reactionary Professor Milosz also found that his own practice as a poet had been reinvigorated by the affirmations of Dostoevsky and especially Swedenborg. Self-destruction versus creative vigor—if the choice was between these two, it was not a hard one.

And yet had Milosz and Swedenborg before him really proved immortality to the senses? Perhaps the ghost of Witkiewicz can, with Milosz's rejection of Weil, rise to haunt him once again. *Selected Poems* as an expression of ecstatic despair is perhaps a far more complex response than that of his early sequence, "The World," but it is open to the same objection. In "Trumpets and Zithers" Milosz wants to identify his ecstasy with the inherent goodness of the world and to identify his despair with his own limitations. But why should we divide things so? Why should we not go the other way? In our despairing moments we are seeing the world as it really is; in our ecstasies we are deluding ourselves, much as Swedenborg was deluding himself when he imagined he had really been transported to the other shore.

Milosz suggests his response to this objection in the very last line of "Trumpets and Zithers": "I thought that all I could do would be done better one day." It is a concession of failure—but he clings to the belief that others will do better in the future. The grounds for this expectation he explored in his next important prose work, *The Land of Ulro*.

The Land of Ulro throughout its first half recreates historically and philosophically the problem with which Milosz was grappling throughout *Selected Poems*. The particular is consumed by the universal; man is but a fleck on the foam of a wave and what matters is the wave not the foam. If Jesus was deluded in prophesying his own resurrection, then the world is a devil's vaudeville bereft of all value. Milosz finds his problem poignantly epitomized in a famous poem by the great Adam Mickiewicz, "The Romantic." Here a village girl "sees" her dead lover and expresses her passionate willingness to join him in death, but at dawn he vanishes and she falls to the ground weeping. The other villagers, though they have not seen her lover with their own eyes, are inclined to believe that he did come, and cross themselves. Such is the sense of presence her words convey. But now two new speakers enter, the first, a scholar:

> "The girl is out of her senses!"
> Shouts a man with a learned air,
> "My eye and my lenses
> Know there's nothing there.
>
> Ghosts are a myth
> Of ale-wife and blacksmith.
> Clodhoppers! This is treason
> Against King Reason!"

The second and final speaker is the poet:

> "Yet the girl loves," I reply diffidently,
> And the people believe reverently:
> Faith and love are more discerning
> Than lenses of learning.
>
> You know the dead truths, not the living,
> The world of things, not the world of loving.
> Where does any miracle start?
> Cold eye, look into your heart!"   (LU, 929)

Mickiewicz asks us to trust faith and love as against lenses and learning. Milosz has come to realize that such a statement of the problem (*pace* Dostoevsky and Shestov) gives up the game. Such romanticism fails because its response is entirely defensive, conceding the world to science and then striving to preserve somehow personal or spiritual values. For Milosz the error of romanticism was what he calls its "insufficient corporeality" (114). It leaves us still the world as science describes it, an inhuman world in which our values have no lasting place. We become citizens of William Blake's land of Ulro:

> They rage like wild beasts in the forests of affliction
> In the dreams of Ulro they repent their human kindness.

The only possible deliverance from Ulro would come from a positive "construction of a vision of man and the world vastly different from that adduced by eighteenth-century science and its modern descendants" (135). This is what Swedenborg and Blake and also Goethe in his scientific writings were trying to do. Each offered a radical alternative to the abstract universe of rationalist science. Each tried to change the direction of what they commonly regarded as the fatal drift of the thought of their times. And each failed, leaving the field to the forces that would alienate, debase, and disinherit us, even within our own consciousness—hence the devil's vaudeville of twentieth-century culture and a humankind "ripe" for its "ultimate reduction," its "metamorphosis into a planetary society of two-legged insects" (157).

Having conceded all this to pessimism, Milosz struggles to find a basis for ecstasy, or at least for hope. He argues that although today Swedenborg, Blake, and Goethe seem like cranks with hopelessly eccentric visions, history shows that the most profound kind of change is possible. If we can be disinherited, then we can be reinstated. Must we choose between God and the truth? Milosz will answer, "For now." Or rather he answers that we need not choose because the opposition may be only temporary. We should embrace contradiction rather than give up something essential to our lives as human beings.

But Milosz has more specific grounds for hope than the generality that everything can change. His specific grounds are suggested by a juxtaposition of the end of the thirtieth and the beginning of the thirty-first chapter of *The Land of Ulro*. Chapter 30 ends:

> I suppose that in the present literary enterprise I am guided, partially at least, by a perverse ambition: can I, by citing an unorthodox tradition, say something about matters I regard as urgent, in a language at once intellectually lucid and evocative, so as to leave an impress on the mind and in that way help to break down the gates of Ulro? (187)

Chapter 31 begins:

> In 1924 a small book by Oscar Milosz was published in Paris under the Latin title *Ars Magna*. It consisted of five chapters or, as he called them, "metaphysical poems," the first of which was written in 1916. *Les Arcanes*, written in 1926 and published in 1927, is both a sequel to and an expanded version of the first book. It contains only one "metaphysical poem," but is appended with a voluminous commentary. (187)

Czeslaw Milosz first met his so-called Uncle Oscar (actually a distant cousin) in 1931 in Paris, at about the time the elder Milosz had become a French citizen after fifteen years of diplomatic work for the Lithuanian delegation to France.[5] Oscar Milosz had long since distinguished himself as a poet in the French language. He was also preoccupied with interpretation of the Bible. In 1932 he discovered what he regarded as the key to the Apocalypse, and he saw ways in which the prophecies of John were being confirmed in contemporary history. In 1938, the year before his death, Oscar Milosz privately published his predictions based on this exegesis.

> The universal conflagration with which the unchaining of the various imperialisms and the basest political appetites threaten us must inevitably unleash, well before 1944, the immense catastrophe foreseen as a punishment by the Prophets and the Evangelists. (*Noble Traveller*, p. 477)

He dismissed his own age as "the age of jeering ugliness, but saw beneath the "disintegrating negation on the surface, a creative affirmation in the depth" (38–40). Milosz was certain about this because on December 14, 1914, after an extended period of isolation in his apartment, he had an epiphany. As he put it to a confidante who came to the apartment shortly after, "I have seen the spiritual sun" (449). In his visionary writings, such as his "Canticle of Knowledge," he exhorted his readers to follow him, to see for themselves this spiritual world:

> You must rise to the Solar Place
> Where by omnipotence of affirmation you become—what?—
>   what you affirm.
> Thus myriad spiritual bodies reveal themselves to virtuous
>   senses.
> First climb up! Sacrilegiously! To the craziest affirmations!
> Then descend, rung by rung, regretless, tearless, with a joyous
>   confidence, a regal patience,
> To that mud which already contains everything with such
>   terrible obviousness and by a necessity so holy! By a necessity
>   so holy, holy, truly holy! Alleluia!   (175)

To those for whom such a flight will seem superhuman or even pathological, Oscar Milosz responds that they should not listen to their reason or even their emotions; as they ascend, it will all seem so natural that it will be as if they were only remembering: "The man in whom this song has awakened not a thought, not an emotion, but a memory, a most ancient memory, from now on will seek love with love" (181). Finding this spiritual memory within yourself, you will also come to know the evil of the world all about you; bearing witness to this evil will then be the visionary's immediate task: "True evil is hidden evil; but once the body has confessed it takes very little to bring the spirit itself, the preparer of secret poisons, into submission. / Like all sicknesses of the body, lepra portends the end of spiritual captivity" (181). So Oscar Milosz can confide his most comforting knowledge: "Thus I learned that in its depths man's body encloses a remedy for all ills" (183).

This hopeful view of our condition is decisive for the later work of Czeslaw Milosz, however often he might protest his own inadequacy to the task. Once again Milosz has based his hope on a visionary experience he has not shared. In *The Land of Ulro* Oscar Milosz personifies no less than our hope for the future. He shows that the Swedenborgian tradition persists into our own time. He shows also that this tradition has some objective foundation in our own nature, for he had reached conclusions much like those of Blake and Swedenborg without having read either.[6] Moreover, Oscar Milosz gives us a concrete notion of how the walls of Ulro might be leveled. His mystical philosophy—developed in some detail in *The Land of Ulro*—centered on his speculations about space. These very speculations he lived to find confirmed in Einstein's theory of relativity, or so he thought. Oscar Milosz hailed Einstein's theory as a liberation of the human spirit, which puts us back on the path of human wholeness, toward a time when scientists and saints will tell us the same truth.

Czeslaw Milosz's claims are more measured. He does not profess to know if Einstein's theory really supports his relative's visionary philosophy (although he clearly regards the parallels as uncanny). He himself wants his readers to share his amazement at something else. More than half a century after meeting Oscar and becoming familiar with his writing in a general way, he has now discovered that his relative's concerns are absolutely central to his own, and might well dwarf anything he himself could hope to do.

Toward the beginning of *The Land of Ulro* Milosz describes its main task as "the story of a man who discovered a treasure in a field and who kept it buried there after failing to turn its riches to profit" (61).[7] The man is himself, the treasure is contained in the writings of Oscar Milosz, and the profit is escape from Ulro. But the escape has not yet come. Oscar Milosz has apparently lost his argument with science as thoroughly as did any of his predecessors. "Mickiewicz lost the argument, as did his more modern comrades, the militant ironists, Dostoevsky among them. But failure was also the lot of those visionary reformers of science, whether it be Goethe, Blake, or Milosz; at best their arguments are of interest only to a chosen few" (240).

Czeslaw Milosz is outspokenly one of those chosen few. But this is different from saying that he knows these arguments to be true, or even that he can make a plausible case from them:

> This much can be said: that Blake's Land of Ulro is not a fantasy if we ourselves have been there; that since the eighteenth century something, call it by whatever name one will, has been gaining ground, gathering force. And all who have sought exit from the "wasteland" (another of the names by which it is known) have been, in my opinion, justified in their endeavor, more, are worthy of admiration, even if their efforts ended in failure and were bought at the price of various "abnormalities." (269)

So he will seem abnormal, not only to others but to himself. Indeed to himself he will not even seem entirely honest: "A man like me, in other words, is constantly visited by a voice imputing his own deficiency as the real source of his internal maneuvers; by a voice which accuses him of *willing* belief in the absence of any real belief. And to this unquitting voice he replies with a mental shrug: So?" (263).

He will persist in his abnormalities, and in what at times seems self-torture. He will persist because of the intensity that eccentric modes of perception—Swedenborg, Blake, Oscar Milosz—give to his imaginative life. He will be an ecstatic pessimist, sharing with Swedenborg and Blake their moments of ecstasy but never himself convinced that these islands of light are anything more than aberrations. He knows them to be beautiful and good, but knows better than to believe that they are true. All that is certain about them is this increased sense of vitality he feels when he is under their spell:

> When my guardian angel (who resides in an internalized external space) is triumphant, the earth looks precious to me and I live in ecstasy; I am perfectly at ease because I am surrounded by a divine protection, my health is good, I feel within me the rush of a mighty rhythm, my dreams are of magically rich landscapes, and I forget about death, because whether it comes in a month or five years it will be done as it was decreed, not by the God of the philosophers but by the God of Abraham, Isaac, and Jacob. When the devil triumphs, I am appalled when I look at trees in bloom as they blindly repeat every spring what has been willed by the law of natural selection; the sea evokes in me a battleground of monstrous, antediluvian crustaceans, I am oppressed by the randomness and absurdity of my individual existence, and I feel excluded from the world's rhythm, cast up from it, a piece of detritus, and then the terror: my life is over, I won't get another, only death now. (246)

He will persist, too, in bearing witness to the possibility of a better time—not a utopia, but simply a day when man's values will be at home in his world:

> My hope, modest as it is, is not addressed to the imminent future. If not the best of worlds, then at least a better one: my renewed civilization will not protect man from pain or personal misfortune, from illness or death; will not free him from the hard necessity of work. But that "most profound secret of the toiling masses, more alive, more receptive, and more anguished than ever," will be deciphered. Man will not be subjected to a fury of words and images designed to make him think in quantitative terms; to make him contemplate others, as well as himself, through an inverted telescope (with a corresponding diminishment, in his own eyes, to something approximating zero). (274)

In the meantime we are destined to live out our lives in Ulro—and so, in conclusion, he pleads: "Reader, be tolerant of me. And of yourself. And of the singular aspirations of our human race." What remains for Milosz the artist is to try to find an appropriate poetic form in which to express these aspirations.

5
The World, Again

What kind of poetry could Czeslaw Milosz legitimately write after his conclusion to *The Land of Ulro?* He could not write the kind of poetry Oscar Milosz had written, for he lacked visionary powers. He could not go back to writing lyrics on Shestovian or Swedenborgian themes; Shestov lacked the ecstasy, Swedenborg the pessimism, of Milosz's mature position. The ecstatic pessimism of *Ulro* entailed a fundamental rethinking of what he sought in his own poetry.

The profound contradiction in the phrase "ecstatic pessimism" is itself suggestive, implying opposed attitudes, voices less in dialogue than in collision. But typically for Milosz, the opposition would never consist of neatly schematic dualities. Reality in the world and in the individual is very different. The word of Ulro is expressed in a babble of voices, for this is a world fallen into fragments. To pretend otherwise, to seek a pure poetic form, is to falsify a condition everywhere full of doubt and ambiguity. To be faithful to reality the poet must let babble into the poem. In fact Milosz, long before this latest crisis, had been drawn to the use of multiple voices in his verse.[1] But never before had he been so conscious of the need for them.

His consciousness of this device—and, as we will see, it was for him far more than a device—was in part prompted by his reading of the critic Mikhail Bakhtin. Anyone who attended Milosz's lectures on Dostoevsky in the early 1970s had to be aware of how important *Problems of Dostoevsky's Poetics* was to him. In this work Bakhtin argues that Dostoevsky discovered "something like a new artistic model of the world, one in which many basic aspects of old artistic form were subjected to a radical restructuring."[2]

The need for a new model arose from an unresolved contradiction in Dostoevsky's own consciousness, one between humanist skepticism and religious faith. Though Dostoevsky might have wished to resolve the contradiction on the side of faith, he could not. The only way to assure that faith had any voice against skepticism at all was to give it a place in a pluralistic world, as one voice among many. Out of this desperate need, then, comes what Bakhtin termed the "polyphonic novel."

Bakhtin does not mean by this phrase a single novel with many interacting and fully developed characters. Great writers had been creating such works for centuries. When applied to Dostoevsky, the phrase signifies a novel in which characters are free from authorial control because the author can offer no overarching point of view to resolve the contradictions he has set forth. Thus all the voices are free to make the splintered claims that issue from their splintered selves. Polyphony in Dostoevsky—both man and novelist—is no more or no less than a reflection of modern reality.

As such it is not simply a device, but an ontological principle. The principle, internalized, explains and justifies the moral torture of the author and his characters in a world so ridden by ambiguity, doubt, and contradiction that no voice can command unequivocal assent; there is no authorial control over character. Dostoevsky cannot be master in his own house. Much as he might prefer otherwise, the voice of the faith he wanted to prevail could not and thus must always endure the challenge and threat by voices of doubt and futility.

This could all seem merely a more intense form of Ulro if Bakhtin had not seen in it a saving grace. This was "carnival laughter," the contradictory play of polyphonic discourse, a joyous sense of the world that celebrates "a mighty life-creating and transforming power, an indestructible vitality" transcending all of our efforts to comprehend it. Bakhtin argues that Dostoevsky's novels, tragic as they might seem, end in a cathartic ecstasy: "nothing conclusive has yet taken place in the world, the ultimate word of the world and about the world has not yet been spoken, the world is open and free, everything is still in the future and always will be in the future" (166). Thus the truly polyphonic work leaves us with "the purifying sense of ambivalent laughter."

From the seventies on, Czeslaw Milosz's most important poetic innovation has been a series of attempts to create his own version of polyphony. The attraction of this enterprise for him should be obvious to anyone who has followed his earlier development. He will, like Dostoevsky, be addressing the central issue of skepticism versus faith, Athens versus Jerusalem. He will concede the apparent superiority of reason and skepticism without abandoning his faith. He will concede the power of Ulro without losing his hope. He will be able to sift through his own remembered past, sift through all of those human things he has watched get swept away by the demonic forces of history, and test their reality through imaginary juxtapositions; for Dostoevskian polyphony is also a test, under combat conditions, of the authenticity of any voice, its power still to speak to us. He will have to submit readily to a kind of moral torture, for he now realizes that not being master in his own house is essential to his artistic vocation. And though he will not experience the unqualified ecstasy of the mystic, in the polyphony of his poetry there will be affirmations in spite of the skepticism: affirmations because there will also be moments of ecstatic experience.

Perhaps because we have come further in divisiveness, have experienced a fuller range of the horrors of Ulro than Dostoevsky could record, Milosz's version of polyphony seems much less an expression of joyous contradiction than of an alert and wary readiness, edged with a suspicion that the voices that sometimes torture, sometimes hearten him are perhaps there to deceive, especially the ones that hearten.[3]

We can observe Milosz working through this complex attitude toward polyphony in a poem of the late sixties called "Ars Poetica?" whose title already introduces an ambiguity that will haunt the poem, in both the question mark and the possible double meaning of the Latin: Is it "*An* Art" or "*The* Art of Poetry"? The first stanza offers no answers:

> I have always aspired to a more spacious form
> that would be free from the claims of poetry or prose
> and would let us understand each other without exposing
> the author or reader to sublime agonies

This "more spacious form" the poet has aspired to implies a profound dissatisfaction with traditional forms of poetry. The dissatisfaction has to do, it seems, with the painful, even embarrassing bathos of the lyric voice. A more spacious form might permit a fuller, less imbalanced expression. So far, so good. This larger form—never described—will then serve as a foil for what the poet is stuck with, mere poetry. And poetry is not just a matter of "sublime agonies" (of the romantic poet?). It also concerns things that the poet might well wish remained hidden below consciousness:

> In the very essence of poetry there is something indecent:
> a thing is brought forth which we didn't know we had in us,
> so we blink our eyes, as if a tiger had sprung out
> and stood in the light, lashing his tail.

This indecency threatens the poet's control, not just over his medium but over his own house. For he is no more inventing voices other than those he might call his own any more than Dostoevsky did. Other voices, therefore, are signs of possession, in the literal sense; symptoms also of the poet's profound ignorance of the sources of his inspiration, a fact that is hardly cause for rejoicing. Or as Milosz has said, "I am a medium, but a mistrustful one" (CCM, 239).

That's why poetry is rightly said to be dictated by a daemonion
though it's an exaggeration to maintain that he must be an
    angel.
It's hard to guess where the pride of poets comes from,
when so often they're put to shame by the disclosure of their
    frailty.

The mocking understatement of these lines, like the question mark of
the title, casts doubt on the whole enterprise of poetry—not that its
forms lack spaciousness, but that it can become the irresponsible
mouthpiece for voices that the poet would rather not think of as his
own. Yet, though they are symptoms of internal disorder and helplessness, he might be perversely proud of them, unless he under-
stands the folly of such pride:

What reasonable man would like to be a city of demons,
who behave as if they were at home, speak in many tongues,
and who, not satisfied with stealing his lips or hand,
work at changing his destiny for their convenience?

The poet, speaking as the "reasonable man" (one voice he asks us to
trust), is shocked by his victimization, his powerlessness to repress
voices less reasonable, which, if he keeps them under control in this
poem, he does at the price of an irony that undermines reason itself.
But in fact, though the reasonable voice can deplore this situation, it
cannot long control it. So much the worse for poets, we might say.
The poet's anguish, however, is no morbid exercise explained by psy-
chiatric textbooks. The poet, working through plural voices, serves
as witness to a permanent predicament of the human condition and
to the present state of the world of Ulro:

The purpose of poetry is to remind us
how difficult it is to remain just one person,
for our house is open, there are no keys to the doors,
and invisible guests come in and out at will.

This is much too emphatic a conclusion for a poet who, following
Dostoevsky, cannot claim that one purpose, his own, controls his

work, when other purposes are clamoring on every side. In the spirit
of the title's question mark, Milosz leaves us with a little self-mocking
mischief, full of implied questions not to be answered, perhaps
unanswerable:

> What I am saying here is not, I agree, poetry,
> as poems should be written rarely and reluctantly,
> under unbearable duress and only with the hope
> that good spirits, not evil ones, choose us for their instrument.

"Ars Poetica?", which begins by confessing to an aspiration to
more than poetry, now admits this poem is not even poetry. Is it
because Milosz enjoyed writing it? Is this what he meant in the first
stanza about sparing his readers and himself sublime agonies? Is he
saying in conclusion that he does not hope that good spirits rather
than evil ones dictated the poem? Why doesn't he hope? Does he
know that evil spirits dictated it? Or none at all? As the title leads us
to a single question mark, so the last stanza leads to an unending
number. We might try to find a single meaning to which this stanza
points, but then we would be ignoring the polyphony of possibilities
that Milosz has ironically sustained here, and the way this polyphony
is itself a witty celebration of possibility.

But we can't help noticing that the celebration is muted, not just
because it must be inferred from contradictory voices—not the sta-
blest grounds for rejoicing—but also because rejoicing must accept a
contradiction so profound that it can never be overcome, at least in
poetry. This contradiction is at the bottom of all the others and can
be summed up: Being, reality, in its wholeness and order is only com-
municable through the fragmentary, partial, and distorting means of
language. How then can the poet hope for anything beyond a hopelessly subjective version of being, made all the more hopelessly subjective by multiplication?

The best characterization of Milosz's predicament in this period is
that of Stanislaw Baranczak: "If Milosz' ontology accepts being, his
epistemology is skeptical: we are not able to reach the essence of an
object—at least we are not able to communicate it verbally to other

people. Because of the mediation of language, every attempt at giving things their names causes a tension between generality and concreteness." Insofar as we can grasp being at all, we do so through a mystical intuition beyond language. The poet then can only use language to take us by the hand and walk us toward the joyous epiphany of being. What techniques are open to him? According to Baranczak, Milosz has settled on two. First, the poet can simply accumulate details, synecdochic fragments, inadequate in themselves but pointing toward the whole. The second technique is to "multiply testimonies belonging to various points of view, value systems, voices—the true Dostoevskian polyphony. Both these techniques share one characteristic approach to the poetic vocation. In both cases the poet's discourse is superior to ordinary discourse not because of its accuracy—he does not have the true name or description, he does not speak in the One True Voice. Rather the poet's discourse is superior by its completeness."[4]

Milosz could now see that the art of poetry he was defending in "Ars Poetica?" was really the justification of his poetic practice from his earliest work. The argument between the woman, the chorus, and the last voices in "The Song" of 1934; "the voices of poor people" of *Rescue* of 1945, as well as the naive voice of "The World"; the bitter depressed poetry of the bleak years of the late forties and early fifties; the joyous whimsey of the period after *Treatise on Poetry*—all could be seen as fragments of a whole. He could now understand why he had been open to such a diversity of influences—Witkiewicz, Weil, Dostoevsky, Swedenborg, Oscar Milosz—why he for a time could make their voices his without betraying his poetic vocation. It remained for him, however, to capture this diversity within a single long poem. This poem is called "From the Rising of the Sun"—and many, including Baranczak, regard it as his supreme poetic achievement.

In this poem Milosz includes not just a plural array of poetic forms, but also extensive prose passages. And in this we may have the most ironic turn of "Ars Poetica?". For the "more spacious form" there can be read as an impossible ideal, a futile effort to transcend the limits of both poetry and prose, serving as a sort of foil for what the poet must actually work with in the real world. Now the question must be asked: Is a poem that combines poetry and prose a realization, however imperfect, of the more spacious form so long aspired to?[5]

Tomas Venclova describes the daunting surface of Milosz's "From the Rising of the Sun":

> It was necessary to respond to questions for which man has no answer, to write when it seemed senseless and intolerable to write, yet also an unavoidable task. In such a situation a poet is justified in using any-thing that happens to fall into his hands—ancient and antiquated forms, echoes from folklore, from the Baroque and romanticism, from primitive syllabic verse, from treatises of the Enlightenment and Greek tragedy. The poetic world is created from fragments of culture.[6]

This poem of almost fifty pages is so complexly textured that the reader is frequently left blinking with incomprehension. The local effects are dazzling, but the effort needed to follow the movement of the poem from section to section is staggering.

We can of course agree with Venclova and simply accept this as the unavoidable consequence of the truly multivoiced poetry suggested in "Ars Poetica?". If we complained to Milosz about our difficulty, we might expect that he would only respond with a shrug that he is just a medium for the confusion of voices. If we persisted in our complaint, he might add that he is a reluctant medium; our complaints are misdirected. He is not in charge.

But more needs to be said about a degree of difficulty that seems to transform the poem from an act of communication into an occult object. Throughout his writings of the mid-seventies, Milosz admits repeatedly that he cannot justify his own practice as a poet; this is the bitter condition of the poet exiled to the land of Ulro. He cannot justify himself, and hence is excluded from the ordinary world of reasonable discourse and comprehensible intentions. In "Oeconomia Divina" (1973) he describes the "unusual moment" in which we live.

The Lord of Hosts has deserted his world; so now everything is permitted, and nothing has meaning. We can take this as the most recent episode in the divine education of the human race ("divine education" is the meaning of "oeconomia divina" in many ancient theological systems). So the poet should sing of God's desertion and eventual restoration, but he must also admit that the hope of an eventual return, for an end to this dark age, seems delusory to the educated mind:

> Neither work nor leisure
> was justified,
> nor the face, nor the hair nor the loins
> nor any existence.   (CP, 236)

In "Temptation" (1975) he confronts this situation, personified as "the spirit of desolation," or rather it confronts him, trying to get him to admit that his own life has made no difference. The poet has no defense, nothing to say in response, except "For Christ's sake, get away from me. / You've tormented me enough, I said. / It's not up to me to judge the calling of men. / And my merits, if any, I won't know anyway" (CP, 324).

This is scarcely an adequate answer, and the question persists: why does he go on writing poetry? The only answer this poem gives is implied by the word "calling," qualified by admission that he makes no claims about his own merits. A fuller response is given in the next poem in *Collected Poems*, "Secretaries," also of 1975:

> I am no more than a secretary of the invisible thing
> That is dictated to me and a few others.
> Secretaries, mutually unknown, we walk the earth
> Without much comprehension. Beginning a phrase in the
>   middle
> Or ending it with a comma. And how it all looks when
>   completed
> Is not up to us to inquire, we won't read it anyway.   (325)

The poet cannot, in fact, justify his practice; he is simply driven to write by voices or a voice, for which he is only the secretary. But how can we be sure that this is the case, that he is a true poet hearing voices, that he is being forced to write by "the invisible thing"? The evidence is that what he writes he does not understand himself; what he writes may make sense, but not to himself or to the present. The legitimacy of his practice as a poet is therefore intimately connected to the obscurity of the poetry, its obscurity to himself and to his readers. (Surely if the readers readily understand the poem, they can't take seriously the poet's claim that he doesn't understand it himself.)

What are we then to make of this claim to be a mere secretary of the invisible thing? We could simply accept it at face value and trust that someday it will all make sense in a worthier age. But another response suggests itself. His claim of helplessness and incomprehension could be a cunning tactic to throw the beasts of Ulro off the scent and to preserve the practice of true poetry across a dark age. If this is so, we should expect that the forbidding obscurity of "From the Rising of the Sun" is only superficial. The labyrinthine surface misleads—is intended to mislead—the citizens of Ulro. It distracts them from a structure that will be clear only to the deserving. If we read "From the Rising of the Sun" as precisely this kind of poem, a deliberately obscure initiation into a final wisdom, in which the poet occupies the role of priest, of mystagogue, the apparent confusion is dispelled. The voices join to make a coherent whole.

But to what is the poet-priest leading us? In the mid-seventies Milosz was still writing on what can be broadly called Sweden-borgian themes. "Proof," for instance, is a description of a Sweden-borgian hell (CP, 326). And it is matched in "Amazement," with its foretaste of the Swedenborgian heaven:

> Innumerable and boundless substances of the Earth:
> Scent of thyme, hue of fir, white frost, dances of cranes.
> And everything simultaneous. And probably eternal.   (327)

(Amid such ecstasy Ulro can only intrude a single small cloud, "probably.")

So it should come as no surprise that near the end of "From the Rising of the Sun" Milosz affirms his belief in the survival of all particulars beyond time, nor that this affirmation is what the whole poem has been carefully structured to bring out. The terms in which this affirmation is made, however, will probably be new to most readers of Milosz:

> Yet I belong to those who believe in *apokatastasis*.
> That word promises reverse movement,
> Not the one that was set in *katastasis*,
> And appears in the Acts 3, 11

> It means: restoration. So believed: St. Gregory of Nyssa,
> Johannes Scotus Erigena, Ruysbroeck, and William Blake.

> For me, therefore, everything has a double existence.
> Both in time and when time shall be no more.

What is new about this formulation is the sense of a doctrinal tradition that reaches back to the Church Fathers and into the Bible itself, although rejection of the *katastasis* of Acts suggests that this tradition might not be altogether orthodox. It began in fact as an attempt of Christianity to come to terms with Hellenism without succumbing to a rationalistic embrace of that thought.

One of the central issues in early church doctrine concerned the survival of human beings after death. For the Greeks this was the immortality of the soul; yet the soul was the rational, universal part of human nature—and hence, when freed from the body, it could lose its individuality and be reabsorbed into the Godhead. Christians, drawing on the apocalyptic tradition of the Hebrew scriptures and on passages such as Acts 3:21, emphasized a bodily resurrection of which Jesus' was the first. At the end of history all will be resurrected and individual bodies restored. Though there was much speculation among the Church Fathers on the differences between these restored bodies and the originals, the body would retain its individuality without being subject to corruption.[7]

But early Christian thinkers like Gregory of Nyssa and Maximus the Confessor were compelled to struggle against the attempt of heretical sects like the Gnostics and Manicheans, whom Weil admired so much, to deny this doctrine and thereby to degrade or even to reject the material world. Orthodox theologians would emphasize the importance of the incarnation as a part of *oeconomia divina,* the divine education of humanity, as exemplified in the bodily life of Christ. So too they would revere Mary as the source of Christ's body, a practice Gnostics regarded with repugnance.

In an early section of "From the Rising of the Sun," Milosz alludes to his lecturing on Maximus the Confessor to undergraduates at Berkeley. Here he was reflecting a new turn in his teaching. He had always insisted on the theological context of Dostoevsky, much to the befuddlement of students who were interested in the Russian as a forerunner of the existentialists and flower children. But now he was developing a course explicitly devoted to theological tradition, a course playfully entitled "Manicheanism Old and New."

There the students would not only read Weil, Shestov, and other moderns who seriously asked what Athens had to do with Jerusalem. They would also be exposed to the intricate twists and turns in the old struggle, both in the ancient and medieval world, between the gnostic and the orthodox: Origen, Gregory of Nyssa, Maximus the Confessor, all trying to preserve belief in the ultimate restoration of all flesh; the Cathari, the Bogomils, the Paulicians, all trying to reassert the ancient heresy.

What Milosz found in this subject was that one persistent battle line between the gnostic and the orthodox was art. Was there a role for relics, icons, and other material objects in the believers' pursuit of spiritual things? Gnosticism, since it rejected the world of matter as unqualified evil, led to iconoclasm, especially to the opposition to the aesthetic representation of historical figures and events. Art was tolerable as allegory perhaps, but not as an attempt to evoke historical particularity, to produce forms that would give value to things of the past.

Manicheanism, old and new. In comparing the old and new, Milosz found that his argument with Simone Weil had already been acted out in an ancient setting. To his surprise, he found that orthodoxy had taken the side of Caliban and had praised the human need to use material things to seek the divine. The world as a land of Ulro

may well have come to resemble hell, but the poet could still seek
salvation within it by finding the divine radiance reflected there—
and he could point this radiance out to others.

Maximus the Confessor, to do this, mastered the *via negativa*. As
he put it: "The perfect mind is the one that through genuine faith
knows in supreme ignorance the supremely unknowable." His own
writing he described as a "theological mystagogy."[8] This is the kind
of sacred wisdom to which "From the Rising of the Sun" seeks to
lead its readers, or at least those readers who deserve to be led. The
title itself bespeaks a covert optimism. It comes from Psalm 113, but is
only part of the full verse: "From the rising of the sun to its setting /
May the Lord's name be praised."[9] We are expected to realize that
this is the psalm always sung at vespers. We are to praise the Lord
even at the end of an eon, for the sun will rise again. So too the last
section of the poem is called "Bells in Winter" and implies the same
imperative; we are still to ring the bells of worship at the barren end
of the year. As he puts it at the end of "Readings," another poem of
this period: "And thus on every page a persistent reader / Sees twenty
centuries as twenty days / In a world which one day will come to its
end" (CP, 234). It is the poet's capacity to see time compressed,
juxtaposed, that enables him to perceive how time can be overcome
and life be made whole. Ulro, seen truly, implies its opposite.

This sense of the juxtaposition of times as leading to the conviction
that time will be transcended in a restoration is captured by a fully
realized lyric embedded near the beginning of the second section of
"From the Rising of the Sun." Here Milosz evokes the concluding
scene of *Issa Valley:* a boy is leaving his homeland in a cart, looking
back to take it all in one last time:

> He sees what I see even now. Oh but he was clever,
> Attentive, as if things were instantly changed by memory.
> Riding in a cart, he looked back to retain as much as possible.
> Which means he knew what was needed for some ultimate
>   moment
> When he would compose from fragments a world perfect at
>   last.   (258)

The boy looks back in space, and the poet looks back in time; he, like the boy, is trying to retain as much as possible; he, more than the boy, knows both how unreliable memory is, yet how all-important. The lyric began: "My generation was lost. Cities too. And nations." And we can also add to that lamentable list a particular item, the life on which the boy is looking back.

The poet knows better than the boy, and hence the irony of calling him "clever." The boy might have intuitively known what was going to be needed for this ultimate moment in which all would be restored; but the poet painfully knows that he cannot compose a perfect world from such fragments. He could only use those fragments to keep alive the hope for a divine restoration, keep it alive across an age during which generations, cities, and nations routinely perished; and the poet himself, as a creature of his age, cannot entirely believe in that hope. This is the vocation of the poet as described in the first section of "From the Rising of the Sun" called "The Unveiling."

The poet begins by confessing that he does not know the why or wherefore of his calling, but he soon moves to what will be the most compelling image of the section: "the dark-blue cloud with a glint of the red horse." The cloud is real, a part of nature; but the red horse is the horse of Revelation, the horse of the apocalypse that will usher in the glorious restoration of the world.

In this image is implied the vocation of the poet as priest, which is to see the glint of the red horse in the ordinary objects around us. In so doing he will be confirming what a chorus in this section calls the "hope of old people." The old people of traditional religion yearn for a "day of comprehension"; they wonder when we will finally reach "that shore . . . from which at last we see / How all this came to pass and for what reason." The poet's task, he knows, is to confirm this hope; but he also lives in an age inimical to it. Even so, his memories return to him, so vividly that he wonders if he had not been called to his vocation before he was born; but at the same time he wonders if putting these vivid memories into words is enough:

Under the dark-blue cloud with a glint of the red horse
I dimly recognize all that has been.

He recognizes, so he writes; but he recognizes so dimly that he writes
"in desolation." And the act of writing itself horrifies him: "Odious
rhythmic speech / Which grooms itself and, of its own accord, moves
on." Thus the poet begins his task. This will proceed by a series of
denials, his own *via negativa*.

The first of these denials is the subject of the second section, "The
Diary of a Naturalist": "I show here how my childish dream was
denied." That dream was a simple unity with nature. Its inadequacy is
suggested by the ironic refrain of this section, "Fare well, Nature."
Nature does not fare well, and so we must say farewell to it. Much as
does the boy Thomas in *Issa Valley*, we in this section outgrow nature
when we realize its brutality: "The lament of a slaughtered hare fills
the forest." Nature is a "callous mother," and the natural world
vibrates with agony. We cannot escape this reality. Even the childish
fantasy of shrinking to live in the world of insects, as does the
fantastic Doctor Catchfly, only increases the horror.

What is left for the naturalist? To escape from nature within it—
that is, to find a holy place free from the struggle for existence. So
"Diary of a Naturalist" ends with an account of a religious pilgrimage
that is largely indistinguishable from paganism. He ends within sight
of "a wooden Madonna with a child in a crown." But this is no good,
for she is surrounded by a "throng of impassive art lovers." To them
she is just a well-made thing, and so he hears no call from the idol. He
concludes that "the holy had its abode only in denial." So we must in
some sense deny the natural, realizing that our homeland is not
within it.

In a poem of 1973, "Tidings" (CP, 237), Milosz identifies civilization with language itself. In explaining this later, he suggested that
we live at two levels—the natural level of the survival of the fittest
and the higher level in which language dominates. It is survival, we
might say, by linguistic selection (CCM, 234–235).

In section three of "From the Rising of the Sun," he attempts naively to effect such a survival for his native land, the area near the little river "Liaude," called by a slight linguistic corruption "Lauda." Of course the slight corruption suggests the futility of the enterprise, as does his continual shifting of languages in this section, from Polish to Lithuanian, to Byelorussian, (and of course from all these to any language into which the poem is translated), with the same object reappearing under different names. The shifting even extends to different dialects of the same language in different areas; and the language, as it shifts, reveals its limitations, its inability to grasp reality.

He struggles to overcome this limitation by sheer detail, as if the quantity of words could make up for their defects in quality. In obsessively long prose sections he tries to describe Lauda, as if with enough detail he could recall the place, bring it back to life. He will even copy out long lists, in archaic dialects, of moveable property from a particular house. The effect of all this is numbing. (He excluded this section from the first English translation.) Yet this obsessive enumeration, as he says at the very beginning, derives from the same need of the human mind that called into being geometry and science. He has tried to understand his world through exhausting verbal detail, and he has failed. He thought "lauda" was a place, but in his failure he finds it to be really a song of praise: "What was accepted in bitterness and misery turned into praise." Praise can yield to poetry. So now having almost lost ourselves in the details of this world, having been once more denied—this time, the refuge of our origins, we finally realize what we must seek: "our unremovable demesne, safe from terrestrial adventure." (After all, the song of praise is for something lost, something no amount or kind of language can restore.)

With these words "Lauda" ends. The next section concerns the first way we might try to escape terrestrial accidents—into the world of pure ideas. But we are given this world from the standpoint of those who oppose it. The poet can never be at home in Plato's republic. So he will begin this attempt to rise above the earth in

"Over Cities," as the fourth section is called, by disavowing responsibility. "If I am responsible / It is not for everything." The poets are
not responsible for Copernicus or the railroads. Milosz protests that
this happened before his time; it did, but it also happened outside the
competence of his craft.

Thus he can present himself teaching Maximus the Confessor to
undergraduates, explaining how Maximus warned against "the devil-
ish temptation in the truth of reason." Maximus was right. "yes, the
Universal is devouring the Particular." Milosz then evokes the world
of the Particular, a sacred place in which a king could enter Jerusalem
riding past green corn, palm in hand. He also evokes the world as it
has become, in which human beings appear no different from a
swarm of insects. Language itself seems incapable of helping, and he
fantasizes about having entered a monastery because "I wanted to
earn a day of comprehension," the same day of comprehension that
was the hope of old people in the first section.

But that hope, as it must be in Ulro, is denied him and he is left
with a sorrowful wonder:

> I was long in learning to speak, now I let days pass without a
>   word.
> Incessantly astonished by the day of my birth, once only from
>   the beginning to the end of time.
> Born of a foolhardy woman with whom I am united, and
>   whom
> I, an old man, pity in my dreams.

He struggles to remember, to call up his mother, but the memory has
faded and he laments: "O what happened and when to *principium
individuationis?*" What happened to it we know, and we are pretty
sure of when as well, though we will soon be shown that more
vividly. For now, his lament, painful though it is, has indeed summoned his mother or her ghost to come to him in darkness. He is
reminded that she, in simple faith, offered him to Our Lady of
Ostrabrama, but he wonders "How and why was she granted what
she asked for in her prayer?" The kind of life for which she might

have prayed was surely not the life lived by the man who is remembering her now. All the lives she might have imagined for him have been snatched away, along with her world, so that he stands alone in darkness. The only redemption here—and it is a very small one—is that he thinks "she has forgiven," for the betrayal of her prayers perhaps.

In the last part of this section, the poet suddenly finds himself in the urbane company of one Hieronymous, a country gentleman of another, older era. In the course of the witty, elegant conversation of this man, and just as "the sun was setting over our land," strange things begin to happen to time and identity: the one speeds up, the other fades. We can read the experience as merely another denial, this one involving the historical death of our land, the old world. Yet such a reading does not quite account for the seemingly unprepared appearance of this figure, and perhaps "Sir Hieronymous" deserves more attention than our brief account has given him.

As knowledgeable a reader of Milosz as Ewa Czarnecka has pressed him on the identity of this allusion, only to be met with polite evasions (CCM, 243). Hieronymous can be identified, however. He is Hieronymous Surkont, the subject of chapter 29 of *Issa Valley*. He was a seventeenth-century ancestor of the boy Thomas, and the original owner of certain strange books Thomas finds in the family library. Surkont was a man of extraordinary complexity, which revealed the historical currents beneath the placid surface of Thomas' world. He was the supporter of a Calvinist prince, although he himself was a Socinian. Surkont and his prince were traitors, on the side of the Swedes in their invasion of Lithuania in 1655; yet they did this in the hope that the Swedes would give Lithuania independence from Poland; so perhaps they were true patriots. When their side lost, Surkont fled, eventually settling in Prussia near Konigsberg, the city later made famous by the great figure of the German enlightenment, Imanuel Kant.

In the novel Thomas' inquiries about Surkont are met with dismissal; Surkont was a black sheep about whom one did not speak. But

Thomas' encounter with him plants a seed that is to bear fruit. Thomas intuitively realizes that the example of Hieronymous proves that, however rooted in time, this place, like any other place, is at the mercy of historical forces hopelessly complex. Confronted with the cosmopolitan life of Surkont, Thomas' own identity, his own self-definition, begins to dissolve. But this absorption into ideas is precisely what the poet is resisting in "From the Rising of the Sun." For this reason he clings to his identity through his mother's following of local Lithuanian custom. When she dedicated him to the most famous Virgin of Wilno, she was performing the ancient role of women as preservers of identity through the body, through matter, much as the old cult of Mary resisted the urbane rationalist assaults of hellenized Christianity. Sir Hieronymous appears as a challenge to that affirmation, for he is a Socinian, a man committed to the most extreme form of hellenized Christianity.[10] The speaker is at first beguiled but, in the end, terrified by the emptiness the conversation leads to:

> Quicker and quicker. A century in half an hour.
> And where is Sir Hieronymous? Where did I go? Here there is
> no one.

So, on this appalling negation, "Over Cities" concludes. And if the poem of which it is a part ended here, there would be good reason to understand "From the Rising of the Sun" as a revision of *Issa Valley*, the jagged, multivoiced poetry of the former displacing the classically balanced prose of the latter. We have now found three allusions from the novel, each one crucial to an understanding of the poem. Then there is the shared concern with various aspects of Manicheanism. But here the difference is critical. For *Issa Valley* is Milosz's most compelling defense of the stark Manichean vision. "From the Rising of the Sun"—as we shall more and more discover—is his most compelling vision of what lies beyond Manicheanism, so that Manicheanism will come to be understood as the greatest temptation to spiritual sin, the one almost impossible for this poet to resist.

But this perception is not yet and the struggle is still defensive, to protest and reassert personal identity against the annihilating gaze of the Enlightenment, against the vacant stare of pure reason. Thus begins the fifth section, "A Short Recess":

> Life was impossible, but it was endured.
> Whose life? Mine, but what does that mean?

The poet's new attempt at meaning is based on romantic sentimentality. He entertains a nostalgic wish to have been permitted to remain in his native place, where he would have grown old, become a respected elder of the region, traveled abroad only on assignment to help his people. He even produces an imaginary conversation between himself, now a distinguished man of the world, and someone honoring him as a distinguished visitor. He lovingly describes his region, tells of how highly learning is honored there, but not so highly "As sack races and jumping over fires / On Saint John's Eve."

The beginning of this section bears comparison to two of Milosz's later lyrics. In "Bypassing Rue Descartes," written in 1980 (CP, 382–383), he rejects the alluring but disastrous rationalism represented by Descartes and the City of Light; and confesses his own guilt for having once killed a water snake, regarded sacred in his district. The message is clear: universal ideas kill; so we must restore abolished customs to their local fame, since human time is not the time of reason. And in "A Felicitous Life" (CP, 322), written in 1975, he describes an old age that resembles what he disingenuously wishes for himself at the beginning of "A Short Recess." The old man finally goes to his rest ashamed of his doubt that the tranquility all around him would last. Two days after his death, a hurricane hits, volcanoes long dormant begin to erupt, and a war starts. As this brief, ironic poem emphasizes, with very good luck one might have an uneventful life, but it is a life lived under an illusion, the stability of the world.

So "A Short Recess" is a little more than half over when the poet confesses that he did not really want to become an old man revered by yokels. "I wanted glory, fame, and power. / But not just in one city of modest renown." His exile, his cosmopolitanism, was necessary to his ambition as a poet. So he ends with self-deprecation that resembles the aporia of "Ars Poetica?" and "Secretaries":

> What if I was merely an ignorant child
> And served the voices that spoke through me?

> Who can tell what purpose is served by destinies
> and whether to have lived on earth means little
> Or much?

He is probably just a medium and does not understand anyway. But this is hardly a rigorous enough way of responding to qualify as a *via negativa*—a shrug of self-serving denial that may do for a short recess but not for a serious session of inquiry.

The title of the next section, "The Accuser," indicates that he will not be allowed to rest in facile skepticism. Milosz may not have been responsible for rationalism, and his childish love of nature may have been inevitable and excusable. But he has no defense against the grievous charge that he was "a gnostic, a Marcionite, a secret taster of Manichean poisons," drawn to its catastrophic myth:

> From our bright homeland cast down to the earth,
> Prisoners delivered to the ruin of our flesh,
> Unto the Archon of Darkness. His is the house and law.
> And this dove, here, over Bouffalowa Street
> Is his as you yourself are. Descend, fire.
> A flash—and the fabric of the world is undone.

To the Accuser this is merely a sign of sin and guilt, "a life spent / In the service of self will." And that service is carried on, if nowhere else, in the poet's adult imagination, where he climbs to a paradisical communion and listens to the preaching of an Albigensian pure one (the kind so admired by Weil): "Revealed to us was the contradiction between life and truth. / In forgetting of earthly years is our movement and peace. / In our prayer for the last day is our consolation." No matter that this voice turns out to be a recording, the poet is convinced and turns in disgust from the world. And this turns out to be self-will, mocked by the Accuser:

In a barber's chair somewhere in a southern city.
Summer heat, jingling, a tambourine.
And a pythoness on the sidewalk
Rocks her swarthy belly in a ring of onlookers.
While here they trim your gray hair and sideburns
O Emperor.
Franz Joseph.
Nicholas.
Ego.

The Accuser also mocks a deeper sin than vanity: "You would like to lead a gathering of people / To a ritual of purification through the columns of a temple." This blindness to the fact that purification is no escape from the world seems almost invincible, so deep is it, so much does the poet wish to become the priest, to shed the material world and attain transcendence. This darkest of sections comes to an end with a series of seemingly unanswerable questions: "A ritual of purification? Where? When? For whom?" This seems to be the poet speaking, as if suddenly wakened to the implications of what has just been said, so that what may seem unanswerable in the conditions of this section, might be answered in another, in which the poet is hopefully awake to his life. And the hint of some hope is already found in the title, "Bells in Winter."

The section begins with a brief narrative. The poet, traveling through high Carpathian passes on an errand for the church, tells of a dream-vision he had, in which a young man appears to him to reveal an ultimate wisdom: "Your truths count for nothing, / His mercy saves all living flesh." This seems to be the doctrine of *apokatastasis,* restoration, which stands against gnosticism that rejects worldly forms. But there is something wrong with the telling. For one thing, the young man in the vision is saved despite the evil he does, as if human conduct in the world means nothing. And the vision seems to be reserved for the few, not something to be shared with the poor and humble. The telling itself is clearly allegorical—the errand through the mountains for the church, the solitary dream-vision. This all, in fact, smacks of gnostic practice, another seduction of

Manicheanism. We recall that allegory is the mode of those who do not believe in the value of history, who preach "forgetting of earthly years." It is no wonder that the poet now dismisses this fiction as a possible but unlived life and dismisses it, it seems, as the last temptation of Manicheanism. But what he will now tell us "is not invention." It is history, his own vivid memory of past experience, recalled to help him argue for something beyond the temptation of spurious dreams and visions.

Here he evokes from memory a real city, his Wilno. He takes us through it, until we finally come to an old servant woman, Lisabeth. She is one of the old people who hope. We watch her as she goes to mass one winter morning, the air suffused with a carmine light, and all the church bells of the city ringing "As if the hands pulling the ropes / Were building a huge edifice over the city." We are with Lisabeth at mass, as the priest says the Latin and Lisabeth follows it in her missal in Lithuanian. And the poet is there with her, to confirm by his intrusions the hope of old people. He first breaks in to explain *apokatastasis,* then twice to wonder about time that seems to dissolve before the power of this (unallegorical) vision.[11] For a few moments he will identify himself with the priest: "As long as I perform the rite / And sway the censer and the smoke of my words / Rises here." From almost a lifetime away he is praising the Lord through the servant Lisabeth (who has been named not after the mother of God but the mother of him who will proclaim his coming). The poet now proclaims the apocalypse. He quotes Blake's *Milton* and alludes to 1755, the date of Blake's birth and Swedenborg's death. The end of our age is coming: "It shall come to completion in the sixth millenium, or next Tuesday." But it will come: "The demiurge's workshop will suddenly be bestilled. Unimaginable silence. / And the form of every single grain will be restored in glory."

This is the affirmation toward which the whole poem has been moving. Yet having made it, the poet collapses. He is still a child of Ulro; he still cannot hope in what he cannot understand. He can understand dark clouds, but not the glint of the red horse. He can understand winter, but not an edifice built in the air by bells. He is more Hieronymous than Lisabeth. So the poem concludes with a single, stark line:

> I was judged for my despair because I was unable to understand
> this.

Had the poem ended with unqualified affirmation, ecstatic pessimism would have been converted into unquestioning, simple faith, a denial of the presence and power of Ulro. The multivocal clash of voices would have ended in a confident solo or a harmonious chorus. But the tentative, personal hope of this poem is discreetly lodged between other lines near but not at the conclusion:

> Perhaps only my reverence will save me.

In this "Perhaps" we are reminded that "From the Rising of the Sun," however affirming, moves on the *via negative* and that this path has no end in Ulro, given the nature of the place.

It should be no surprise that in his next major poem, "The Separate Notebooks" (1977–1979), Milosz is still in a state of ecstatic pessimism, opening himself to other voices almost to the point of aesthetic anarchy. His model seems less "From the Rising of the Sun" than the section of it he titled "Lauda," in which long prose passages alternate with verse. It is as if in this mix he has found the "more spacious form" alluded to in "Ars Poetica?" as an aspiration—except that he and his readers are not spared the "sublime agonies" that form should transcend. Notebooks, after all, are a writer's diary and must be ready to record whatever deeply matters to the writer, even personal agony, if that proves to be grist for the mill. And it does, for ecstatic pessimism is nothing if not a personal response to Ulro and the condition of the self therein.

Presented as a selection of entries, poems, and prose from a private journal, "The Separate Notebooks" is meant to give the impression of a mind in spiritual crisis, haunted by a legion of contradictory voices, each demanding a hearing, all urging some fragment of a whole, never, it seems, to be grasped. Each entry develops some aspect of the torment in this experience. For example, the opening poem of the first section is a third-person account of a quest begun in hope and ending in failure. The questor, an "old man, contemptuous, black-hearted," is a persona of a Milosz who has let the pessimism overwhelm the ecstasy. The old man metaphorizes his experience as a dream that leads through "halls full of mirrors"—a house of solipsistic ego—and "all around him the voices are intoning." We hear in this yet another version of the poet-scribe of "From the Rising of the Sun," compelled to record these voices because "he wanted, once, to understand his poor life."

The next entry records a first-person meditation on the Sacramento River and on ships, "black animals among the islands," innocent of the writer's disillusioned and incommunicable knowledge of what life holds out. The next entry, in prose and the third person, relates a ghost story; the ghost is a Polish gentleman who cultivated detachment from the world but found that "petty angers and ill feelings and family quarrels are so durable that they force us to walk after our death." Neither surrender to nor renunciation of desire seems to bring resolution to the spirit. The ghost story is interpreted by another entry, a first-person poem in the voice of the old man, which begins

> I did not choose California. It was given to me.
> What can the wet north say to this scorched emptiness?

California is desolation, arid space, "dried-up creek beds." The answer to the pessimism of the opening question is the question itself, translated at the end into the terms of ecstasy:

> Where is it written that we deserve the Earth for a bride,
> That we plunge in her deep, clear waters
> And swim, carried by generous currents?

In the imaginative act of filling the dried-up creek beds with deep waters we learn the dangerous power of art, aesthetic fulfillment while the world itself is lost. By the end of the ghost story, resumed after the poem, we have learned that detachment, in any case, is probably not possible to humans.

Thus the reader is prepared for a new voice, that of Cézanne uttering his dreadful judgment: "Le Monde—c'est terrible." But this judgment, from a man whose revenge on the world was to turn it into an aesthetic object, only serves as an obdurate challenge to the old poet looking for resolution among contradictions. He counters Cézanne not by argument but through an example, the memory of three real people, long dead, now summoned to Cézanne as "witness to my grief," the grief at the loss of the ecstatic present.

There is Gabriella, beautiful in her youth, now an old hag. And Eddie, athletic and handsome, dead by his own hand. And Mieczyslaw, the artist who used them as models, executed for hiding Jews during World War II. It is his dilemmas that stand for the dilemmas of all kinds of artists. Even as he tries to preserve them, he "takes" lives by turning them into aesthetic objects. He loses his own life and artistic future by engaging in the world of desire and action to save the lives of others. So can the poet. The words with which he celebrates life are dead abstractions, the actual life sacrificed for aesthetic beauty. The actual life, even his own, is sooner or later defeated and destroyed by time. It is no wonder then that the last line of this poetic section of the entry is a final half dismissal of the great French painter: "And it is bitter to sing in praise of the mind, Cézanne." At this point the entry becomes a prose meditation in search of some compromise between ecstasy and pessimism, unbridled desire and aesthetic distance. Thinking about the three figures in vivid detail gives him a kind of comfort, and he concludes with a deeper consolation based on an *a fortiori* argument for God's presence:

> He thinks that the word *past* does not mean anything, for if he
> can
> keep those three so strongly before his eyes, how much
> stronger than his is an unearthly gaze.

Yet Cézanne's challenge is only a foretaste of a much more powerful one embodied in Schopenhauer, who appears in the next (prose) entry, not through any obvious logic but characteristically by a deeply felt connection, the connection of apparent opposites:

> A portrait of Schopenhauer consorts, who knows why, with a portrait of Ela who, adorned by the painter with a Renaissance hat similar, probably, to those worn by ladies on the deck of the *Titanic,* smiles enigmatically.

Schopenhauer's power lies in the clarity and depth of his description of the Miloszian dilemma: "No one had ever so forcefully opposed the child and the genius to the rest of them, always under the power of the blind will, of which the essence is sexual desire." Addressing the philosopher, the poet insists that, under all the precision and logic of Schopenhauer's language, his "only theme was time: A masque on midsummer night, young girls in bloom, ephemerid generations born and dying in a single hour. You asked only one question—is it worthy of a man to be seduced and caught?" The answer of Schopenhauer (and Cézanne) would, of course, be nō.

The next entry is Milosz's own answer, a sort of prose poem about lovers waking in the morning, "dazzled by themselves and by their part in the earth of the living." They see, as they walk down into a valley, two towers and hear the "thin voice of a little bell." The sight of "That cloister, small cars high above it on the road," and the hearing of an "echo and then silence" seem to bring them to "a revelation—what kind they don't know—because it will never advance beyond its beginning."

Milosz here shifts into prose, rebuking Schopenhauer for being "too severe for their short-lived élans of the ego." But he concedes to the philosopher the accuracy of his description of the aesthetic experience, quoting (in italics) the philosopher's own words on the loss of the self, where one "is pure will-less, powerless, timeless subject of knowledge." Milosz has experienced this, felt its temptation. His response at first might seem odd. Instead of opposing the philosopher with some self-affirming lyric ecstasy, he offers as the next entry another prose poem describing a naked, burnt-out landscape, in the midst of which is a museum that preserves, of all things, the pathetic artifacts of nineteenth-century European royalty. The narrator finds the contrast too much:

> What madman chose this place to dispose the souvenirs of his
>   adoration
> lilac-colored scarves and dresses in crêpe de chine?

The madman, as the next prose passage tells us, is the American millionaire, Sam Hill, who chose this place on the desolate border between central Washington and central Oregon to build a museum honoring his friend, the beautiful princess Maria of Romania. This bizzare, wildly out-of-place testimony to "adoration," though hardly an answer to Schopenhauer, is not easily dismissed. The work of a madman, true, but it also stands for all efforts of passionate desire to save something of beauty from the desolation of time. In this sense it is an absurd parody of poetry. Milosz responds to it first in a poem that registers wonder and quiet despair at trying to comprehend it or anything because there "is too much world"; then, in an intense prose passage where he seems to surrender to desire, "staring at the face of every woman passing in the street. Wanting not her but all the earth." But this settles nothing, for the very next entry is a poem spoken by a woman who accuses all the intellectualizing talkers—Milosz among them—of failing to understand "how to think about the dead." Like the voice of nature itself, she accuses them of missing the essential point: "all the rest remains" after their talking is done. Their words do not comprehend, let alone touch, experience nor does nature mind their words, after which, and in silence, the truth manifests itself:

> The scent of winter apples, of hoarfrost, and of linen:
> There are nothing but gifts on this poor, poor earth.

Milosz responds to her sad affirmation with a prose description of a "dark Academy," where all the elegant euphemisms are taught, the multiple ways of talking around fleshly experience: "In reality there is only a sensation of warmth and gluiness inside, also a sober watch-fullness when one advances to meet that delicious and dangerous thing that has no name, though people call it *life*." If Schopenhauer seems here to be dismissed in favor of something people call *life*, "sober watchfulness" is hardly a triumphant (or comfortable) stance.

The remaining poems in this section of "The Separate Note-books" work through an anguish over inadequate language (with which to describe the past) and personal shortcomings, to celebration grounded on the prosaic reality the poet has faced. He is smitten with wonder at all he has learned, an amazing mix of good and evil:

> Pure beauty, benediction: you are all I gathered
> From a life that was bitter and confused.

But the wonder is not felt only as a blessing, for "How can laments and curses be turned into hymns?" Doubts and terrors persist:

> And why all the ardor if death is so close?
> Do you expect to hear and see and feel there?

Yet the intellect does not have the last word here, for

> the lips praised on their own, on their own the feet ran;
> The heart beat strongly; and the tongue proclaimed its
>   adoration.

Milosz has conceded to Schopenhauer that individual lives are ephemeral, that the world can be terrible, but "what a show it is! / In the hall of pain, what abundance on the table." And to Schopenhauer's unspoken question about his own passing, Milosz responds with a shrug, almost blithely,

> So what, if, in a minute I must close the book:
> Life's sweet, but it might be pleasant not to have to look.

So this section ends with a celebration of ecstasy, however precariously sustained.

But how does one go on sustaining celebration against the weight of human history, which trivializes the present with the all-but-impenetrable expanse of the past? Milosz shows how it can be done in "Pages Concerning the Years of Independence," the brief second part of "The Separate Notebooks." He is writing about this twenty-year period of 1919–1939 when Poland was an independent state. Yet into these few pages of poetry and prose entries he manages to weave in references to a vast range of Polish history, in another effort to restore the past.

He begins by trying to imagine himself back into that time of independence, no simple task—"It is much easier to reach the Columbia River which empties into the Pacific, or to pitch a tent at the Athabaska River flowing to polar lakes, than to penetrate that zone marked by the zigzag silver lines on the collar of his father's uniform." But he can remember fragments from that time, which his imagination connects with fragments from other times. He is continually reminded of lines from a nineteenth-century poet, Juliusz Slowacki, lines from his *King Spirit* that recount the emergence of the Polish spirit in the middle ages and the rekindling of Polish nationalism in the nineteenth century. Milosz's thoughts now turn to the war that destroyed the Polish nation. He considers what was lost then and personifies the loss in Josef Czechowicz, killed at the outset of the war, a young poet whose work made clear a deep continuity between traditional and modern poetry and between folklore and high culture.[12] Milosz addresses Czechowicz, wondering if there is any point in talking to him at all: "It is possible that the dead do not need reports from the Earth, and see in one symbol all that occurred later." Such a symbol for what occurred later (and before) is, of course, what Milosz himself is seeking in his "Pages Concerning the Years of Independence." Milosz assumes that the ghost of Czechowicz, like the ghost in the earlier story, will still have some concern, at least about his own continued earthly existence in the memories of those he left behind: "Yet I presume you have some trace of interest, at least as to your own continued stay among the living." But Czechowicz is only one of a group of tragic figures of the time, the hopeful and gifted, lost to exile and death. A brief catalogue of the lost evokes the war as a whole. "That creaky office on Dabrowski Square disintegrated. Before you perished from a bomb, Szulc in Auschwitz, Szpak from a bullet because he refused to be closed in the ghetto, Janina Wlodarkiewicz from a heart attack in New York."

As this passage evokes the war as a whole, so "Pages Concerning the Years of Independence" evokes much of the spirit of Polish national history. If Slovaki's poem represents the Polish middle ages and before, Slovaki himself represents the nineteenth century and Czechowicz represents the period of the early twentieth up to World War II; and Milosz represents that war and its aftermath. The point here is that, as with individuals and nations, whole eras of national life are subject to the same erosion and annihilation. At the end of these few pages, this compressed vision of the nation, Milosz can return to his central opposition between ordinary desire and the detachment of art. He poses the problem to Czechowicz: "Lives taken away, lands defiled, sins: and your note, pure above the abyss." Czechowicz has achieved that detachment; he has become his poetry. "But only the chant endures, nobody knows about your sorrow." Now Milosz can formulate his problem in a way that combines both the personal and the historic, speaking as if he himself were already dead, as if he existed only through his poetry: "And this is what tormented me in those years I lived after you; a question: Where is the truth of unremembered things? Where are you behind your words, and all who are silent, and a State now silent though it once existed?" To this question Milosz devotes the third and last section of "The Separate Notebooks."

In the first part of "The Separate Notebooks" Milosz asserts the primacy of desire over aesthetic detachment. In the second part he presents the years of independence and Polish history as something alive with desire, which can never be reduced to an aesthetic object. In the third section he has to inquire into the status of all that had never been captured in a work of art, all that is doomed to be lost to human memory. Milosz, were he not a denizen of Ulro, could at this point summon traditional religious consolation. The soul of Czechowicz, unforgotten by God, awaits the resurrection of his body during the last days. All joys and sufferings are recorded forever in the Book of Life. In our time, though, such consolation has lost its authority. But what is "our time"?

"The Wormwood Star," the title of the last section of "Separate Notebooks," is another allusion to the Apocalypse: "And the third angel sounded, and there fell a great star from heaven, burning as it were a lamp, and it fell upon the third part of the rivers, and upon the fountains of waters. And the name of the star is called Wormwood: and the third part of the waters became wormwood; and many men died of the waters, because they were made bitter" (Revelation:10–11). This is our time. And it is accursed—accursed not just because of the triumph of science and materialism, but also because we no longer believe in the truth of unremembered things. This failure of belief confines us to the prison of a meaningless present. For us, Czechowicz no longer exists behind his words. Even the living "are an echo that runs, skittering, through a train of rooms." This is bitter news for those who want to be something more but hardly believe they even exist.

Those among us who have lost most are often those doomed to be most haunted by what was lost. Another name for this condition is greatness. Another still, exile: "that's how my prayer of a high school student was answered, / of a boy who read the bards and asked for greatness which means exile." The imperative of this particular kind of greatness, exile, is to record one's memories lest their truth be lost forever with the loss of the rememberer.

The process begins, the polyphonic babble of a nightmare: "He hears voices but he does not understand the screams, prayers, blasphemies, hymns which chose him for their medium." Here we are in the presence again of the poet-scribe of "From the Rising of the Sun" and the old man in the opening of "The Separate Notebooks." He begins to recall in great detail his own past—Red Cross tents "on the shore of a lake at a place called Wyshki," "his beautiful cousin Ela" riding along a battle front "with a handsome officer, whom she has just married," the glitter on epaulets reflected from the fire in which, his mother has told him, "if he looks long enough he will see a funny little man with a pipe in there, riding around."

Milosz's obsession with details puzzles him. Why must he get them right? No one would know if he changed a detail here and there. All he knows—taking the dictation of the voices—is that this is his duty. Despite the fact that "he does not understand," some of the memories make clear prophetic sense, for example, one especially vivid memory of a train ride taken as a young man. Through his sleep in the cold empty car he hears all the noises a train makes. "He wakes up, rubs his eyes, and above the tossed-back scarecrows of the pines he sees a dark-blue expanse in which, low on the horizon, one blood-red star is glowing." This, strangely, is a consolation. For prophetic vision, however dire, indicates an order in things, an order that transcends human comprehension. Just as the early Christians, under the persecution of emperors like Nero and Diocletian, found comfort in the apocalyptic visions of John, so Milosz finds comfort—bitter though it may be—in such visions as are still possible in the modern world. The last poem of this section, and of this work, is called "The Wormwood Star," and it conflates times in such a way as to make our world, cursed by the scientific world view, another version of Diocletian's Rome:

Under the Wormwood Star bitter rivers flowed.
Man in the fields gathered bitter bread.
No sign of divine care shone in the heavens.
The century wanted homage from the dead.

They traced their origin to the dinosaur
And took their deftness from the lemur's paw.
Above the cities of the thinking lichen,
Flights of pterodactyls proclaimed the law.

They tied the hands of man with barbed wire.
And dug shallow graves at the edge of the wood.
There would be no truth in his last testament.
They wanted him anonymous for good.

The planetary empire was at hand.
They said what was speech and what was listening.
The ash had hardly cooled after the great fire
When Diocletian's Rome again stood glistening.

If we are still in the eon of the Gospels, then suffering is not merely historical, but human. This conclusion seems to give the final word to Schopenhauer and his various personae. What ecstasy is possible under Wormwood? Perhaps even Schopenhauer's pessimism was not stern enough. For how is aesthetic detachment even possible now for those sensitive enough to experience it? Moments of joy and its celebration are overwhelmed by boundless suffering and evil, are lost in the anonymity of the "planetary empire." Except that the final word on the planetary empire is the poetry Milosz here makes of it.

In its first English publication in book form (1984), "The Separate Notebooks" is set among poems that reinforce its polyphony.[13] In the prose poem "Esse" the poet recounts a ride on the Metro and his ecstatic feelings in the presence of a lovely young woman, his fellow passenger. She exits at Raspail and he continues in despair:

> I was left behind with the immensity of existing things. A
>   sponge,
> suffering because it cannot saturate itself; a river,
> suffering because reflections of clouds and trees are not
> clouds and trees. (7)

In the next poem, "Ode to a Bird," ecstasy thrusts despair into the background:

> But your half-opened beak is with me always.
> Its inside is so fleshy and amorous
> That a shiver makes my hair stand up
> In kinship with your ecstasy.
> Then one afternoon I wait in a front hall,
> Beside bronze lions I see lips
> And I touch a naked arm
> In the scent of springwater and of bells. (11)

Toward the end of the volume, we find a haiku-like record of a moment, if not quite ecstatic, full of undoubting wonder at experience:

> Transparent tree, full of migrating birds on a blue morning,
> Cold because there is still snow in the mountains. (197)

A few pages later, "Account" bitterly begins: "The history of my stupidity would fill many volumes" (203).

But it is "Reading the Japanese Poet Issa (1762–1826)," the last poem in *The Separate Notebooks,* which perhaps most elegantly plays out the polyphonic contention that dominates the book. "Reading" is a poetic commentary on three poems by the Japanese poet (quoted in the commentary), the first of which opens

A good world—
dew drops fall
by ones, by twos.

Milosz elaborates on these "few strokes of ink" and then tells us that "Poetry can do that much and no more," because "we cannot really know the man who speaks." The consolation offered by Issa is severely limited, as if "it subsisted / by the very disappearance of places and people." The price of such aesthetic distance is that it must dehumanize and generalize the world. Then the second Issa poem:

A cuckoo calls
for me, for the mountain,
for me, for the mountain.

This is an occasion for Milosz to imagine the actual poet, like Milosz himself, doubting: "how is it that the voice of the cuckoo / always turns either here or there? / This could as well not be in the order of things." Milosz has restored what Issa has suppressed, the human behind the poem. But the cost of this restoration is high, for the human immediately questions his own aesthetic conclusions about the world, whether or not the order of poetry has anything to do with the order of nature.

The third Issa poem is much closer to Miloszian polyphony:

In this world
we walk on the roof of Hell
gazing at flowers.

Here ecstasy and pessimism are combined in such a way that they are parts of a seamless vision. It is Milosz's turn to affirm in his qualified way:

> To know and not to speak.
> In that way one forgets.
> What is pronounced strengthens itself.
> What is not pronounced tends to nonexistence.
> The tongue is sold out to the sense of touch.
> Our human kind persists by warmth and softness:
> My little rabbit, my little bear, my kitten.

What is affirmed is twofold: animal warmth and the power of the word to preserve it in memory. And then this final passage:

> Anything but a shiver in the freezing dawn
> and fear of the oncoming day
> and the overseer's whip.
> Anything but winter streets
> and nobody on the whole earth
> and the penalty of consciousness.

This conclusion renders the affirmation that precedes it very fragile, the result perhaps of fear, of the possibility that Issa's unpeopled landscape may actually be the hell of desolation itself.

Once again it may seem that Schopenhauer has the final word or, if he does not, his pessimism still so hedges us in that any hard-won affirmation is all but lost in despair. All but lost, yet not quite. The old man of "The Separate Notebooks" has kept his unspoken vow, to be relentlessly honest, and has been rewarded in the end with a small boon—the belief that words might preserve living warmth. If ecstasy has not been saved by the book's quiet ending, the poetry that treats it as a subject has been saved. And that much under the Wormwood Star is considerable. In an accursed world, however, poetic saving may not be enough.

Milosz had two public occasions in the early 1980s on which to test the small, cautious affirmation reached at the end of "The Separate Notebooks," and also to argue for the polyphonic character of true art. One occasion was his response on receiving the Nobel Prize in

1980; the other was his Charles Eliot Norton Lectures at Harvard in
1981–82. A public address is usually a summons to affirm certain
values, shared by speakers and audiences, whether the occasions
themselves celebrate some triumph or lament some defeat or death.
The question both these occasions posed for the poet was how to
make a public affirmation on the grounds established in "The Separate Notebooks," how to make an affirmation that contained its own
negation. Poetry (even mixed with prose) was one thing. Prose
oratory was quite another, though both modes might urge the same
attitudes.

To be an effective orator, Milosz had to persuade his audience not
that poetry was important—the occasions assumed this—but that it
was important in a way that might at first seem eccentric. To be an
honest orator, he also had to admit the difficulties his view faced, not
the least of which was his own penchant for pessimism on the one
hand and, on the other, his penchant for the ecstatic. If the first
attitude would have somehow undercut both occasions (and also
been boringly like the attitudes of most other living poets), the
second might appear unseemly in a man of his age and place in the
world of letters.

In neither presentation does Milosz slight his pessimism, though
he never lets it win the day. And in both he modulates ecstasy down
to the phrase "quest for reality," his definition of the poetic vocation.
Milosz's readers, however, would know that this phrase meant a
good deal more than what it might seem to express on the podium.

In his Nobel Lecture, he asserts that the quest for reality is never-
ending because earth in all its multifarious particularity can never be
encompassed in words. A poet leaves a trail of poems behind him,
"like dry snake skins, in a constant escape forward" (NL, 6). But the
poet has a competitor in the task of encompassing the world, in our
day a highly successful competitor: ideologies that have achieved
their ends through the "uniform worship of science and technology."
The competition is unfairly one-sided, since science and technology
have served to give us nothing less than dominion over nature. This
dominion, however, has not been simply of humans over nature, but

also of humans over humans and has been achieved "at the expense of millions of human beings destroyed physically and spiritually" (8).

Perhaps in Western Europe this destruction of the human spirit occurred too gradually to be noticed, but for someone from the "Other Europe" it happened within a single lifetime. Milosz's Lithuania was not one of those places where the "traditional bond of *civitas* has been subjected to a gradual erosion, and their inhabitants become disinherited without realizing it." Lithuania was a place that persisted in its "disorderly illogical humanity . . . an indulgent anarchy, a humor disarming fierce quarrels, a sense of organic community, a distrust of any centralized authority." It persisted until "suddenly all this is negated by the demoniac doings of history, which acquired the traits of a blood thirsty deity" (9).

But what is a poet to do who has witnessed this negation and has intimately known its victims? He cannot rest content as a poet in the classical sense. For literary classicism, from its heights, ignores the misery; the price of aesthetic distance and formal purity is to lose one's common humanity. No longer can one aspire to fly above the earth and look down: "The Earth which the poet viewed in his flight calls with a cry, indeed, out of the abyss and doesn't allow itself to be viewed *from above*. An insoluble contradiction appears a terribly real one, giving no peace of mind either day or night, whatever we call it: it is the contradiction between being and action, or, on another level, a contradiction between art and solidarity with one's fellow men" (11).[14]

Here we have the concession to pessimism. The poet comes face to face with juggernaut history that threatens to crush him and whatever value his art attempts to throw up in defense. But history, recent history, is in some sense only an agent of time, which is the real enemy of being and art. The poet's pessimism is only a current manifestation of a deeper, more ancient problem, a more ancient pessimism: "Reality calls for a name, for words, but it is unbearable, and if it is touched, if it draws very close, the poet's mouth cannot even utter a complaint of Job: all art proves to be nothing compared with action. Yet to embrace reality in such a manner that it is preserved in all its old tangle of good and evil, of despair and hope, is possible only thanks to distance, only by soaring above it—but this in turn seems then a moral treason" (12).

Here again is the dilemma of the painter Mieczyslaw. It is an ancient dilemma made intolerably intense by modern history, "the contradiction at the very core of conflicts engendered by the twentieth century and discovered by poets of an Earth polluted by the crime of genocide" (12). One has to realize that using poetry to escape the horrors of the twentieth century, to get above it, is to be complicit in those horrors. Milosz certainly sympathizes with any poet who wants to escape history, who wants to be "elsewhere, in other countries, on other shores, to recover, at least for short moments, his true vocation—which is to contemplate Being" (14).

His choice of the phrase "other shores" is significant. He seems to have found a positive way to account for his own partial failure as an erstwhile Swedenborgian. Of course he wishes, as any true poet would, to escape to the other shore and be able to contemplate pure being. And he had some moments, gifts of respite, when he did know what such distance would be like. But in the twentieth century, persistence in pure contemplation from "above" would be little less than moral treason.

Even so, what alternative is left for the poet who wishes to remain a poet? Polyphony is one answer, but Milosz thinks there is another: the poet can play a public role, countering in concrete terms the erosive effects of his powerful competitors. The domination of science and technology has weakened our sense of history. "We are surrounded today by fictions about the past, contrary to common sense and to an elementary perception of good and evil" (15). More than a hundred books have been published which deny that the Holocaust took place; and countless others treat the Holocaust as belonging "to the history of the Jews exclusively, as if among the victims were not also millions of Poles, Russians, Ukranians, and prisoners of other nationalities" (16). The poet then can use his linguistic gifts to bear witness to a past that others would deny, rationalize, or distort. Poets, especially poets from the other Europe, can be the bearers of memory for western civilization. And here Milosz finds a way to make endurable, if not to resolve, the contradiction involved in the poet's vocation, especially in the twentieth century.

The difficulty with the original formulation of the problem was the word "above." It seemed to suggest a willed, spatial detachment, the poet flying away on linguistic wings. Claiming to be at once here on the earth and there in the contemplative heavens was an insoluble contradiction. But if the problem is reformulated in temporal terms, much that is contradictory in the poet's vocation can be resolved. The two terms are no longer "here" and "above," but rather "now" and "then." The contemplative "above" becomes the remembered "then." Milosz bears no responsibility for being removed in time from the Lithuania of his youth. No one bears moral responsibility for the passing of time.

But isn't a poetry of memory as much a poetry of moral escapism as a poetry of contemplation? Can a poetry of memory be anything more than an exercise in aesthetically refined nostalgia? To such objections Milosz has a remarkably simple answer.

Our moral obligations are to people. How are we to exercise those responsibilities to those no longer alive? We must remember them, keep them alive in all their particularity through our memories. We struggle then against "the mystery of time" which, left to itself, will "change events, landscapes, human figures into a tangle of shadows growing paler and paler." If we do not struggle, the past will become an empty abstraction, of service to those who would impoverish the present. "Those who are alive receive a mandate from those who are silent forever. They can fulfill their duties only by trying to reconstruct precisely things as they were and by wresting the past from fictions and legends" (22). In preserving the past, poetry renders its greatest service to the present.

The occasion for affirmation provided by the Nobel ceremonies is not one to inspire rhapsodic rhetoric. Much of the literate world is looking on, listening for serious wisdom from those chosen out of a vast multitude of talents, the most excellent among the excellent. Milosz's response was to meet the occasion on its own terms, to offer a moral position for the artist, an engagement not with the politics of his day but with the reality of a value that we are losing every day and every second. "What is not pronounced tends to nonexistence" (CP, 332). And this is sufficient. What beyond moral duty, beyond a sacred pact with those who are gone, drives the poet to recapture the past in its wholeness, to encompass its multifarious particularity? The poet does not say. Perhaps there was no reason to, on this platform. Pessimism was given its due and, against its background or in its context, poetry had a firm place. If the poet awoke to ecstasy on the morning of his address or passionately remembered his own lost kin, the uncle, say, who set him on the road to Stockholm, he does not say. Ecstasy may be better found in action, in experience, and in a poetry that hints of being.

The affirmation Milosz expressed in his Nobel Address was more fully developed in the Harvard lectures in the next year. That podium gave him a more ample space in which to examine the role of poetry in the world, poetry, as his title affirms, as witness. But the kind of witness requires some context. This he gives in six lectures (revised for publication), which position him geographically, historically, and as a member of the tribe we call poets, especially in their modern form. Readers of the poet will recognize old themes here (and the familiar dramatis personae): above all Milosz as the inheritor of a complex, contradictory history that all but ends in the catastrophe of the German invasion and its long aftermath. As a Pole and—to make matters even more complex—as a Lithuanian, he lives on the borderline between many opposing powers, best summed up in the opposition of the new world to the old.

But this opposition is not simply temporal. It goes deeper into the core of how humans perceive the world. For example, he poses literary classicism against his own kind of realism, a realism emerging from conflicting voices. As he had argued in the Nobel Lecture, classicism remains silent about misery, a misery that poetry ignores at the cost of its humanity. Poetry must continually struggle against the distancing powers of form. And this calls for a mixed style, a dialogic interaction between suffering humanity and classical formalism.

This dialogue is invigorating, a continuous (if often painful) celebration of life. It is for this reason that he finds himself also in profound opposition to the prevailing gloom of modern poetry. The lesson of biology (the title of the third chapter) has taught us that a providential cosmos is a mere projection of desire against an infinite background of natural processes governed by necessity and chance. The reaction of most poets to this lesson has been despair and a progressive withdrawal from the great human family, as an act that "goes against the grain of our civilization, shaped as it is by the Bible and, for that reason, eschatological to the core" (WP, 37).

Milosz himself is eschatological, that is, a poet who cannot accept or, worse, enjoy a poetry of hopeless pessimism and despair. Yet even this kind of poetry—the despairing poetry of our own age—is not to be taken lightly; there are other and deeper reasons for it than "the separation of the poet from the great human family." Among these are "the progressing subjectivization that becomes manifest when we are imprisoned in the melancholy of our individual transience; the automatisms of literary structures, or simply of fashion" (115). These produce a poetry that, while basking in its own malaise, also bears witness to the spiritual sickness of our time.

Oscar Milosz had written that "poetry has always followed, fully aware of its terrible responsibilities, the mysterious movements of the great soul of the people" (quoted, 25). His relative, Czeslaw, now infers, "Thus the state of poetry in a given epoch *may* testify to the vitality or to the drying up of the life-giving sources of civilization" (34). But this scarcely seems to support Milosz's argument against despair, for twentieth-century poetry (with a few exceptions) could hardly be more bleak. Milosz prefers to interpret the pessimism of modern poetry in a different way. He will interpret it polyphonically and find an affirmation at the heart of its despair:

> Yet it is one thing to live in a limbo of doubt and dejection, another to like it. Certain states of mind are not normal, in the sense that they turn against some real, not imaginary, laws of human nature. We cannot feel well if we know that we are forbidden to move forward along a straight line, if everywhere we knock against a wall that forces us to swerve and

to return to the point of departure, in other words, to walk in a circle. Yet to realize that the poetry of the twentieth century testifies to serious disturbances in our perception of the world may already become the first step in self-therapy. (17)

Such a healing will require a return of the conviction that "behind the interplay of phenomena there is a meaningful world structure to which our hearts and minds are allied." Of course in the twentieth century everything "conspires to destroy that supposition, as if it were a remnant of our faith in the miraculous" (53). And perhaps we have only entered an inferno from which there will be no exit. We might think, looking at our own time and its poetry, that there is no exit and that pessimism deserves to win the day. But for the eschatalogical poet, the story does not end there, in some inferno.

Characteristically, Milosz finds grounds for hope in the midst of despair, at the scene of one of the great crimes of the twentieth century. In "Ruins and Poetry" (chapter 5) he finds the ultimate place to test hope and a poetry that can affirm without falsifying our experience. The place is Warsaw under Nazi domination. If poetry had proved a superfluous lie or an invitation to hopelessness, it could not have survived in such a place, in such circumstances. But it did flourish and to this day provides a witness, not just to its own validity but to a time of heroic struggle and, perhaps more important, a time of drastic simplification. The moment-to-moment danger, the deprivation, misery, and fear brought on by the war and invasion reduced life to its essentials. As it turned out, for the victims, the oppressed, poetry was one of the essentials—not usually the poetry of art, or classical detachment, but, at its best, a poetry of realism, one that embodied what our own poetry lacks: a sense of hierarchy when appraising phenomena; a sense of value, of what comes first in the basic struggle for life. "All reality is hierarchical simply because human needs and the dangers threatening people are arranged on a scale. No easy agreement can be reached as to what should occupy first place. It is not always bread; often it is the word" (96).

It has to be conceded that the simplification brought about by catastrophe did not lead to the kind of hope that the culture of the old world, the world now in ruins, had promised at its most optimistic. The poet who wanted to affirm, to transcend pessimism, had now to do so out of the fragments of his own life and what was left of his culture.

> The poetic act changes with the amount of background reality embraced by the poet's consciousness. In our century that background is, in my opinion, related to the fragility of those things we call civilization or culture. What surrounds us, here and now, is not guaranteed. It could just as well not exist—and so man constructs poetry out of the remnants found in ruins. (97)

But are these ruins in fact not signs of an inferno from which there is no exit? We cannot be wholly sure. Yet in the metaphor of simplification through the fires and suffering of war, another place is signified, one of purification. It is thus that Milosz can suggest that our age might be "a purgatory in which the imagination must manage without the relief that satisfies one of the essential needs of the human heart, the need for protection" (209). Perhaps this purgatory will result in a new world view, one that will not reduce mankind to cosmic inconsequence. Milosz here turns prophet:

> Daring to make a prediction, I expect, perhaps quite soon, in the twenty-first century, a radical turning away from the Weltanschauung marked principally by biology, and this will result from a newly acquired historical consciousness. Instead of presenting man through those traits that link him to higher forms of the evolutionary chain, other of his aspects will be stressed: the exceptionality, strangeness, and loneliness of that creature mysterious to itself, a being incessantly transcending its own limits. Humanity will increasingly be turning back to itself, increasingly contemplating its entire past, searching for a key to its own enigma, and penetrating, through empathy, the soul of bygone generations and of whole civilizations. (110)

The best way to prepare for such a world view is with a poetry that "connects the time assigned to one human life with the time of all humanity" (37). He does not deny that the struggle between development and disintegration "may very well end in the victory of disintegration. For a long time, but not forever—and here is where hope enters. It is neither chimerical or foolish. On the contrary, every day one can see signs that now, at the present moment, something new, and on a scale never witnessed before, is being born: humanity as an elemental force conscious of transcending Nature, for it lives by memory of itself, that is, in History" (118).

These words close *The Witness of Poetry.* Though they are hopeful, they are not confident. Poetry cannot with certainty witness the future, even if it is eschatological or prophetic. It can only testify to and for its own time—and thus redeem the fading present for the future, and the faded past for the present. Indeed, Milosz's view of poetry is necessarily backward-looking, historical, however much the history is tangled with the individual life of the poet. Testimony after all is a record of what someone has once touched, seen, heard, smelled, or tasted. It is a record—however dim—of real pleasure and real pain, reality itself, the ecstatic moment, about which Milosz, given this occasion, says little. He leaves his audience on a high level of abstraction—"elemental force," "transcending Nature," "History"—more at home in the discourse of philosophy or historiography than that of ecstatic poetry.

But if his audience at Harvard went out and bought the lectures in book form, they would find something added—a poetic epigraph at the beginning. It is the lyric "From the Rising of the Sun" in which a young boy (and the poet through him) looks back upon the native land he is leaving, looks back somehow realizing that in some ultimate moment he would have to compose from these fragments "a world perfect at last." This is the witness of poetry. We must look backward for perfection in some unstated future.

In *Unattainable Earth* (published in both Polish and English in 1986) Milosz includes a preface that serves to guide the reader's expectations. "Why not," he rhetorically asks, include in one book, along with my own poems, poems by others, notes in prose, quotations from various sources and even fragments of letters from friends if all these pieces serve one purpose: my attempt to approach the inexpressible sense of being? Such a design I adopted in this book, searching, as I have once said, for "a more spacious form." And I hope that under the surface of somewhat odd multiformity, the reader will recognize a deeper unity. (UE, xiii)

We are more likely to recognize this unity if we have been following the poet's experiments with polyphony, with the "more spacious form" he identified in "Ars Poetica?". The quest for unity in multiplicity is carried on here, with a vengeance—over thirty voices, ranging from brief quotes from the Gospel of Mark to a long letter from a friend, and including whole poems by Whitman and Lawrence as well as the poet's own voice in different modes and moods.

Although *Unattainable Earth* is more relentlessly polyphonic than either "From the Rising of the Sun" or "The Separate Notebooks," the themes found in the earlier poems constitute those of the new book, and all are grounded on the basic Miloszian theme: the "attempt to approach the inexpressible sense of being." No one charm will capture this unicorn, but perhaps a variety of them will, a variety that will somehow correspond to the multiformity of being manifest in human experience—and not just in the experience of many voices but in the experiences these voices try to project.

Thus we have the familiar juxtapositions of past and present, here and there, of momentariness and a sense of the eternal, becoming and being. Thus the old poet of *Unattainable Earth* will remember and relive the beginning of all his "voyages in dreams," modeled

> in one, very real, by a cart from Raudonka on the
> Wilno-Jaszuny road for a kermess in Turgiele. A
> sandy road with ruts, always either up or down,
> stubble fields on hills in the sun, here and
> there a spruce grove, then alders by streams, huts,
> well-sweeps.   (untitled, 53)

This lone sad dreamer is the boy who will become the young poet of catastrophic pantheism, still rhapsodically alive within the old poet:

The city exulted, all in flowers.
Soon it will end: a fashion, a phase, the epoch, life.
The terror and sweetness of a final dissolution.
Let the first bombs fall without delay.   ("The City," 60)

And this is the young poet, who as a boy flirted with Manichean heresy and now as an old poet, circling back to his beginning, concludes that the only explanation for human suffering is to assume

The existence of an archetypal Paradise
And of a pre-human downfall so grave
That the world of matter received its shape from diabolic
    power.   ("Theodicy," 113)

Like Yeats in "Among School Children," Milosz finds reality not in one time or place, not in one person or voice, but in a totality, a simultaneity. The first epigraph of the book is from Montaigne: "Our life consists partly in folly, partly in good sense; whoever writes on it only in a staid fashion and with measure leaves more than half of himself behind." Recording one's own folly and good sense could, of course, seem like an exercise in egotism. But contradiction is still a principle of human experience, and thus being sometimes can only be understood by living through contradictions: "Captive of my sensual nature, only through lovemaking was I able to experience myself dissolving in communion, alive among the living. A triumph of the 'I' (was it not?) allowed me to break out of the enclosure of the 'I'" (89).

If there is a fundamental difference in this book from the earlier ones, it is the emphasis on the joy in ecstatic pessimism. There is energy in the exercise of pessimism itself. He approvingly quotes Pascal: "Denying, believing, and doubting completely are to man what running is to a horse" (79).

It is not that the despair engendered by pessimism is gone from this book: "Man never had a clear representation of life after death. But now, when the priests and the faithful say the words 'life eternal,' no representations appear at all" (78). But *Unattainable Earth* begins with a paeon to "The Garden of Earthly Delights." True, this paradise is soon enough lost to demonic powers, but the final pages express gratitude and quiet joy:

> Yes, this is a plenitude I searched for. Found not in books of philoso-
> phy, or on church benches, or in flagellating myself with discipline.
> After a day of varied activities, to feel at dawn my oneness with
> remembered people, despite a thought about my person separated
> from others. (136)

This satisfaction is, however, not forgetful of its ground and limits:

> "My parents, my husband, my brother, my sister."
> I am listening in a cafeteria at breakfast.
> The women's voices rustle, fulfill themselves
> In a ritual no doubt necessary.
> I glance sidelong at their moving lips
> And I delight in being here on earth
> For one more moment, with them, here on earth,
> To celebrate our tiny, tiny my-ness.   ("Myness," 133)

They cannot, in the nature of things, get him much beyond the evidence of personal experience, which, powerful as it is, requires the experience of others to extend and complete it, to give adequate voice, that is, to a world beyond personal experience. And so Mark, Augustine, Buber, Baudelaire, Goethe, Shestov, Weil, Saisho, and the rest—the dominating presence of voices whose tone is more often on the side of ecstasy than not. This explains the prominence of Lawrence and Whitman in *Unattainable Earth*. These poets fre-quently composed in some ecstatic mode. But, more important, they also found their reason for ecstasy in the erotic, and it is the erotic on which Milosz bases his own ecstatic stances in *Unattainable Earth*.

It is no wonder, then, that Casanova gets as much space as Pascal in the book. No wonder either that Milosz envisages salvation as a union in "what we have in common: the same nakedness in a garden beyond time" (18), or that the book contains a poem beginning "I liked your velvet yoni, Annelena, long voyages in the delta of your legs" (21). But the erotic is not confined to human lovemaking. Oscar Milosz and Swedenborg are quoted to show that God's relation to his creation is also sensual. The longest prose excerpt is not a painful message from Dostoevsky (who is nowhere mentioned) but rather a fable from Vladimir Soloviev (123–125). It tells the story of two monks who succumb to temptation, indulge themselves with abandon in the brothels of Alexandria, and then try to return to their ascetic life. One monk feels remorse for his sins and finds he can no longer live the holy life; fully abandoning himself to debauchery, he dies a damned man. The other denies having done anything wrong, claims to have spent his time in Alexandria piously, and ultimately achieves sainthood: "When the day of his death arrived, his withered and emaciated body, as if blooming with beauty and youth, became radiant and filled the air with fragrance." Even sanctity, the parable seems to be teaching, is rooted in the joyful, unashamed acceptance of sensuality.

If this new erotic emphasis seems distant from Dostoevsky's, it accords with the polyphonic motif as described by Bakhtin; for polyphony leads to the carnival world in which all is permitted. (Bakhtin's other major study is on Rabelais.) Milosz himself seems to feel liberated into the carnival world by the extreme polyphony of *Unattainable Earth*. One brief quotation succinctly explains why. Significantly, it occurs not in any of Milosz's own writings but in a private letter sent to him on March 4, 1983, by Joseph Czapski. The postscript of the letter reads:

> Please do not be surprised that in a letter written for you and about you, I feed upon quotations. I find in them *an answer* such as I wouldn't be able to find myself, so now I live on quotations and they rescue me. "*Lorsque on ne s'efforce pas d'exprimer l'inexprimable, alors rien ne se perd et l'inexprimable est contenu inexprimablement dans ce qui est exprimé.*" [When one does not force himself to express the inexpressible, nothing is lost and the inexpressible is contained inexpressibly in what is expressed.]—L. Wittgenstein. We do *not* know: perhaps it must be so, we do not know anything about the value of that which we give—it is *inexprimablement contenu dans ce qui est exprimé.*

The relief that this recognition must represent for Milosz is already present in the first section of *Unattainable Earth*, "The Garden of

Earthly Delights." The paradise that Milosz evokes here, based on Hieronymous Bosch's triptych, is not an abode of unmixed happiness, where lion lies by lamb. It is a place of animal appetite, of monstrosity, *and* of Adam's dazed wonder at a situation he cannot yet and may never understand, much like the condition of Milosz himself. The poet can identify with both Adam and Eve, with the man who "contemplates with incomprehension" and the woman, "the mysterious one." He ate of the tree of knowledge, was exiled from Eden, and, as fallen Adam, feels her pulse in him at night, her "mortality. / And we have searched for the real place ever since" (6).

The real place is the earth, described in the central panel of the triptych. The scene, as the poet renders it, is filled with innocent sensuality, the world of Eros, a surreal world where Adam and Eve "bite into wild strawberries bigger than a man." The sensual joy of the creatures seems boundless (and sometimes comically grotesque) in its variety and is without shame or guilt; to suggest a higher approval, "a flock of lunar signs fills the sky / To prepare the alchemical nuptials of the planets" (7).

It is significant that Milosz's next poem is called "Earth Again" and does not take up the subject of the triptych's right panel usually thought to represent hell. Instead, the poem celebrates the things of the world, but almost as an illusion, a lure or temptation for amazed Adam:

> They are incomprehensible, the things of this earth,
> The lure of waters. The lure of fruits.
> The lure of two breasts and the long hair of a maiden.

All this and much more—so that "for a short moment there is no death / And time does not unreel like a skein of yarn / Thrown into an abyss."

There the series ends, but the next poem is a sort of postscript, as its title "After Paradise" suggests. Here the poet tries to comfort Adam and Eve, waking them in "a royal bed by a garret window," raised above the bitterness of earth, two happy lovers living fully in their moment of love, which transforms "the street of tall peeling porticos."

This tender respite leads into "The Hooks of the Corset," a prose passage. Adam (now the poet-witness) observes the evanescent multitudes of the big city, dressed in strange costumes (the latest fashion). He experiences their joys directly by becoming one of them and by imaginative power: "I multiplied myself and came to inhabit every one of them separately, thus my impermanence has no power over me" (10). But why this odd if intriguing title? it has no direct reference in the poem. The answer comes a little later, after a prose passage of Baudelaire's on Constantine Guys, a man also avid for a life to be found "wherever the natural man and the man of convention show themselves in a strange beauty, wherever the sun witnesses the hurried pleasures of a *depraved animal*." Milosz dreams himself (again in prose) back to Paris in 1900, a lover, perhaps like Guys, coming to an assignation (why not? Adam is Everyman). He is engaged "in a serious operation" and "for that reason released from the reproach of shirking my social duties." Preparing to make love, he finds the operation all but accomplished:

> On the verge of a great discovery I almost penetrate the secret of the Particular transforming itself into the General and the General transforming itself into the Particular. I endow with a philosophical meaning the moment when I helped her to undo the hooks of her corset.

The corset is what presses the bulges of the body into shapely form and, unhooked, releases the flesh for its fulfillment. Corseted form (as in classical poetry) is the general, whereas the freed body (as in reality) is the particular. Thus in the act of unhooking the corset, of undressing a lover, Milosz finds momentary resolution of a contradiction that has haunted him almost from the beginning of his career.

On page after page of *Unattainable Earth,* Milosz strives to follow the exhortation of the *Corpus Hermeticum,* to

> think that you are everywhere at once, on land, at sea, in heaven. Think that you are not yet begotten, that you are in the womb, that you are young, that you are old, that you have died, that you are in the world

beyond the grave; grasp in your thought all this at once, all times and places, all substances and qualities and magnitudes together; then you can apprehend God.

This is no less than a summons to the poetic imagination, and Milosz continuously responds to it in words—his own and others'—that try to escape corseted forms.

It would be vain to seek schematic development in these efforts to imagine out of or beyond himself, efforts to find the inexpressible contained within the expressible. The dialogic play of form and reality, of justice and the world, desire and fulfillment (or failure of fulfillment), does not lend itself to orderly development, but to a dramatic interchange of positions, each trying to contain or under- mine the others, with the occasional interjection of a cry of joy or (less frequently) of weariness with the process. But sensuous joy predominates:

> What will the poetry of the future be, which I think of but will never know? I realize it is attainable for I experienced brief moments when it almost created itself under my pen, only to disappear immediately. The rhythm of the body will be in it, heartbeat, pulse, sweating, menstrual flow, the gluiness of sperm, the squatting position at urinating, the movements of the intestines, together with the sublime needs of the spirit, and our duality will find its form in it, without renouncing one zone or the other. (33)

In the very prophecy (rendered in prose), what is prophesied is in part realized. Yet in Ulro the duality remains not simply a duality but also a cruel contradiction, tearing the self in two and away from otherness, separating language from reality, art from truth.

The two themes, the unattainable earth and the expressible word that would make it inexpressibly attainable, everywhere determine the "formless" form of the book and the poet's judgments of himself, and they drive him—as did the summons from the *Corpus Hermet- icum*—to go on imagining far-off places and times. These themes both elicit and explain his fundamental attitude toward life and his place in it. "What use are you? In your writing there is nothing except

immense amazement." But beyond this amazement, the naive amazement of Adam, is the poet's relentless avidity for Eve and for the reality he often believes shines through her. It is as though, if he entered
experience and individuality deeply enough, he would come out on
the other side, in universality—the old pantheism, but now touched
and humanized by personal love. He imagines himself through primal experience back to where "I was guided and protected by Eros,
and whatever I was doing grew immense, standing in front of me,
here, right here." Eros is the presiding spirit of the *Unattainable
Earth*. The book treats sexual love in its various forms, from lust to
tender care. Eros is the divinized personification of the poet's passionate attachment to the world of things, the force that moves him
to find reality in the particular loved thing.

Eros, however, could also be deception. In "From the Rising of
the Sun," Eros deceives us with beauty:

> Should we then trust
> The alchemy of blood, marry forever the childish earth of
>   illusion?

The answer there was no. Now it seems we have no choice unless we
want to destroy the world, standing high above it   as if we could
to administer justice. It seems that, as always, we must seek to
embrace the world, while a detached part of our mind reminds us
that the seeking most likely is a snare and perhaps fatal, since Eros
cannot explain sin and suffering except in the most impersonal terms
of the urge of the individual or species to reproduce (Milosz's account with Schopenhauer has by no means been settled).

Just as there is no rest for the wicked, so there is no durable stance
for the polyphonic poet. Every voice is provisional. Perhaps the only
solution is to move with the motion of things. But how is this
detached acceptance possible for a poet to whom simplicity is the
reality, the essence? It is exactly this simplicity that he cannot reach.
The carefree and compliant spirit he recommends here is hard to
maintain when one's whole being strains toward grasping at the
unattainable.

Near the end of the book, in "The Poet at Seventy," he sums up his life, jestingly addressing himself as a theologian, and poses once more, but not in jest, the old contradiction—his love of the immediate sensuous experience of earth and his need for something enduring beyond such experience:

> Thus, brother theologian, here you are,
> Connoisseur of heavens and abysses,
> Year after year perfecting your art,
> Choosing bookish wisdom for your mistress,
> Only to discover you wander in the dark.

His failure is humiliating but

> On this sad earth no time to grieve,
> Love potions every spring are brewing,
> Your heart, in magic, finds relief,
> Though Lenten dirges cut your cooing.
> And thus you learn how to forgive.
>
> Voracious, frivolous and dazed
> As if your time were without end
> Your run around and loudly praise
> *Theatrum* where the flesh pretends
> To win the game of nights and days.

But the end is futile:

> And all your wisdom came to nothing
> Though many years you worked and strived
> With only one reward and trophy:
> Your happiness to be alive
> And sorrow that your life is closing.   (139–140)

Here, at an age where he had expected wisdom to bring him certainty and peace, he finds only the same old avidity for the earth, the sad earth full of suffering and of what perishes. Yet in its beauty it gladdens him. Eros is still at work. The love elixir is, of course, what brings on enchantment and delusion. If the penitential fasting of Lent (which is after all a preparatory work of spring) teaches him forgiveness, he is eager for the reborn earth and its theatrum of the

flesh and of change, happy to plunge into its midst again. But at least
he is undeluded in his delusion, knowing full well that the fashions
hiding and decorating the flesh (and what is inexpressible in it) are
not of nature. Is this, then, the last word? Not quite—never quite.

The last piece in this book is a brief prose summary of the relation
of the poet's art and human fate, almost something that could have
come out of a notebook or a diary, part wish, part ideal, part description of the fact:

> To find my home in one sentence, concise, as if hammered in metal.
> Not to enchant anybody. Not to earn a lasting name in posterity. An
> unnamed need for order, for rhythm, for form, which three words are
> opposed to chaos and nothingness.

If we recall that form has been reduced to style, to fashion, we might
wonder how form—along with the rhythm and order that compose
it—can be trusted to oppose chaos. But here we must remember the
"more spacious form"—not an aesthetic stylization of experience,
but a mode open to contrary voices and movement. That mode,
Milosz believes, is as close as we will get to finding the essence *in*
experience. If this sounds like Schopenhauer again, there is an important difference. The form Milosz aspires to is not Platonic perfection,
not a corset for experience. Miloszian form should include all the
elements of human contradiction the poet describes in his prophecy,
compelling us to see both flesh and spirit, time and eternity, as one
thing, one indescribable thing, attainable, but not now—or if now,
only for a grievously short moment.

This condition summons forth the new Adam in the old poet,
whose deepest response is primal wonder, the wonder that contains
all other voices in the book, contains and unifies them not by reduction to one transcendental or abstracting voice, but by acknowledg-
ing the one in the many, the simple in the complex, Eve in all women.

> How could I have expected that after a long life I would
> understand no more than to wake up at night
> and to repeat: strange, strange, strange, O how strange,
> how strange. O how funny and strange.   (136)

6
Milosz
Collected

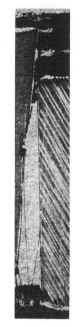

In 1988 Milosz published a work that might seem to demand a radical revision of his poetic career as seen through the eyes of his readers in English. This is *Collected Poems,* consisting of poems already translated into English, a number of older poems not translated before, and a group of new poems at the end of the book. But the new or newly translated poems fit comfortably with what is already familiar to us, in ethos, matter, and manner. Turning to poems like "Early Morning," composed in 1976, is like coming upon an old friend in fresh garb:

> Galloping horses
> Of the departed century.
>
> Day breaking,
> Huge, over the world.
> My torch fades and the sky glows.
> I am standing by a rocky grotto above the hum of the river.
> In the dawn radiance on the mountain a sliver of the moon.
>
> (CP, 345)

In a ritual older than Christianity, the speaker greets the dawn of a new day in wonder and in the primal company of the four elements.

If there is need for revision, it does not come from the addition of new poems. But what about the more drastic change, the reordering we find in *Collected*? For Milosz the editor has submitted Milosz the poet to chronology and presents the poems, so far as possible, in the order of their original appearance. Thus the previous books of poetry in English have undergone subtraction, addition, rearrangement, and in one case, *Selected*, dissolution to give the poems their proper place in the history of the poet's development.[1]

The latest stage of this continued development is represented in the new work added to *Collected*. "New Poems, 1985–1987" consists, as do all of Milosz's earlier books, of loosely connected individual poems and one or more serial poems, where each individual section (which can be a poem, a fragment of a poem, prose, or a mix of poem and prose) serves the larger whole. The center of gravity for "New Poems" is the serial poem "La Belle Epoque," which stands to its book as "From the Rising of the Sun" stands to *Bells in Winter* (or, in *Collected*, "From the Rising of the Sun") and as "The Separate Notebooks" stands to the book of that name (or, in *Collected*, "Hymn of the Pearl"). Like the other major serial poems, "La Belle Epoque" mixes verse and prose, admits multiple voices, and crosses personal fate with history, in this instance, an era that proved to be a gorgeously fevered conclusion to a whole world and its values.

The first section of the poem, "The Trans-Siberian Railway," opens with poetry, an autobiographical fragment from childhood:

> On the Trans-Siberian Railway I travelled to Krasnoyarsk,
> With my Lithuanian nurse, with my mama; a two-year-old
>   cosmopolitan,
> A participant in the promised European era.
> My dad hunted marals in the Sayan Mountains,
> Ela and Nina were running on the beach in Biarritz.   (463)

This ironical glimpse of little Czeslaw being groomed for a world on the edge of death peters out into a prose description of the *belle époque,* as if the subject were almost too farcical for poetry: an absurdly optimistic dream set against a terrible reality. The dream was of "a truly European and even cosmopolitan epoch." Already "French novels in yellow covers were read on the Danube and the Vistula, on the Dnieper and the Volga. McCormick harvesters were working in the fields of the Ukraine." In 1913, when the poet was "a two-year-old cosmopolitan," the dream already seemed a splendid reality, heralded by the poets, one of whom composed "La Prose du Trans-Siberian." The nineteenth-century revolution in transport was the event that seemed to bring the dream into actuality, though it brought other things too.

At this point the poet imagines himself at one with his father. He becomes the individual he knows as his father, who is hunting in the mountains, a vast distance beyond the borders of civilization; and then he becomes Ela of the opening stanza, who is running toward the waves or standing naked and lovely before a mirror, touching her breasts, suddenly illuminated, suddenly knowing secretly and forever that all the gauds and masks of culture, all that is *belle* about the *époque,* is false.[2] "How good it is to touch oneself and not to believe them even a bit, and everywhere, in the sun, in the white clouds above the sea, in the rustling of the waves, in one's own body to feel this: completely different" (464). This feeling of difference (in prose that has become quietly poetic) is the joyous expression of nature, the pure sensuality hidden under culture, and stands in silent rebellion against the concealing arts of culture. But the rebellion stops with the individual; it has no political consequence and is ultimately crushed by time and suffering.

"Beyond the Urals," the next section, is a verse debate precisely about politics, a debate that occurred on an eastward-bound train that Milosz's mother, pregnant with Czeslaw, was taking to join her husband in Siberia. The argument is between an archeologist, Valuev, and one Peterson. Valuev the pessimist asserts that "Nobody wants the truth. Man cannot bear the truth." And he mockingly recommends that his opponent "take refuge / In the incense smoke, in icons, in priests' chantings." But nothing will change the fact that "what lasted for centuries is perishing," and no amount of shaman magic will "wake the Killed One" or prevent the end in which "a song of mourning" will be mistaken for "a triumphant song" and "lofty thought says: 'Let what's destined to fall, fall. / Let the new race receive the gift, its mortality. / Let it rule the earth, dance upon ruins" (466).

Peterson's rejoinder is a sneer: "That's teenage melodrama." He then prophesies the birth of a great new age when not just religion but also philosophy and art will be gone, everything born from fear of death. The people of the new age will become gods, given immortality by science. We are meant to recall here the suicidal visionary Kirilov in Dostoevsky's *Devils,* and perhaps meant also, as the prophecy gets wilder, to see in it a science fiction version of Christian orthodoxy:

> The promise will be fulfilled, the dead will rise.
> We will bring back to life our father, thousands of generations.
> We will populate Mars, Venus, and other planets.

And citizens of the new age will be good because it is our mortality that makes us behave badly. To this Valuev answers a dismissive "Ha!" A brief prose comment notes that Peterson's argument is based on the writing of Nicholas Fedorovich Fedorov (1828–1903), who believed that science would give humans immortality and that our duty would then be to revive all our ancestors. Then another brief note: "Both Valuev and Peterson were executed in 1918." So the voices of extreme pessimism and extreme optimism are silenced by a new voice that incorporates both views in a supreme contradiction of boundless hope and brutal necessity.

The coming of the new age is described in the next section, "First Performance," where the orchestra is tuning its instruments to perform *The Rite of Spring,* the famous first night of Stravinsky's revolutionary ballet (1913). The god of the new age, as embodied in this music, is Dionysius, glimmering "olive-gold, among the ruins of Heaven," replacing the "noble-minded rabbi who announced that he would live forever / And would save his friends, raising them from the ashes." The cry of Dionysius, "of earthly ecstasy, is carried by the echo in the praise of death" (468). This seems like yet another version of ecstatic pessimism.

From poetic intensity and vision we are led into the matter-of-fact prose of "The Northern Route" in the next section, a literal-minded treatment of the transportation revolution. It seems that in the summer of 1913 (fatal year), Fridtjof Nansen, the Norwegian explorer, sailed on the vessel *Correct,* following the northern route from Norway to Siberia, with the idea of finding a more economic way of transporting goods than by railway. Nansen's book on the voyage— an argument for sea transport—is quoted. Thus what was to spread culture is now going to spread commerce and an unspoken political and military power. But in all this practical concern for economic development—dry and abstract—the poet, moving into verse, catches a glimpse of the men on the deck of the *Correct,* Norwegians and Russians, among them the poet's young father, and we are for a moment caught up in the eternal present of the individual. But this vision is quickly lost, replaced by memory of the photograph that is the source of the vision, a photograph that

> hangs in our apartment in Wilno,
> Five Podgórna Street. By the jars
> In which I rear newts. What can happen
> In ten years? The end? The beginning? of the world.

It is too much:

> What a confusion
> Of times. And places. Here I am, uneasy,
> In the midst of California spring, for things do not fit together.
> What do you want? I want it to exist. But what? That which is
>   no more?
> Even your newts? Yes, even my newts.[3]

And in this the poet goes the crackpot Peterson one better—not just his ancestors but all life, all things restored to baffled life. What a confusion indeed. Between little Czeslaw the cosmopolitan and the old poet in Berkeley, time and place have lost their meanings. And the confusion is in no way relieved by the next section, "Revolution-aries." This opens with a paragraph from Nansen's book, this time not about the vast developmental possibilities of Siberia but about political exiles, their endless boredom, and we may be reminded that we are in the territory of *The House of the Dead*. The Nansen quote is followed by poetry that zooms in on these exiles, "noble revolution-aries" who "look at the Yenissei current" (the very river Milosz's father hunted by), "Read *Das Kapital*, yawn, wait." They wait for the man-god (of Peterson's prophecy), for the lucid mind, which will be "as clear as two and two make four." And we are surely to remember at this point that there is another kind of computation, the rebellious math of *Notes from Underground*, where the sum of two and two is not necessarily four because life does not add up so tidily. But the man-god will not be distracted by such distractions. He will take vengeance and educate, he will impose obedience until his people "lose the human nature in which they take refuge, / Though it does not exist. Til / their mask falls off / And they enter the heights, transformed by agony" (471). At this point both Valuev and Peterson appear utterly innocent, and it is no wonder they were to be swal-lowed up by the power of the man-god. The question is: transformed into *what* by agony?

This ghastly vision of the spirit of the new age is followed by what looks almost like frivolous relief, a paragraph that the poet Blaise Cendrars clipped from a Paris newspaper and included in his "Inedits secrets." This clipping is a little catalogue of pretty young women, prostitutes one assumes, named as they pass "through the cafe hall" and vanish "at the staircase leading to the first floor." The last woman is Jeanne, who appears "in a hat adorned with one red plume," a touching after-glimpse of the *belle époque* disappearing before our very eyes, while we are still thinking of the coming of the man-god, of whom we were told: "Compassion is not his hobby."

The final section, "The Titanic," like the climax of a tragedy, involves a catastrophe. The section begins with the testimony of a witness to the sinking of the *Titanic*,[4] John B. Thayer, who insists that, despite other disasters, we were living in a dream of peace until this one and then, "the world of today awoke April 5, 1912." The poet then meditates in prose on disasters, those well publicized and those not, the latter sometimes far more terrible, such as "the Russian-Japanese War. There is no reason to wonder, as even passengers on the Trans-Siberian Railway a few years after 1905 did not think of thousands and thousands of the killed rolling in the muddy currents of the river Amur." Among those passengers, we know, were Milosz's mother, Valuev, and Peterson. Here prose shifts to poetry, as we are given a closeup of the end of the *Titanic,* the only sound of collision "a feeble rasp"—a faint signal of great catastrophe—suggesting the fragility of the *belle époque* and its works. The poem concludes with the hymn played by the *Titanic* band as it sank, beginning "God of mercy and compassion" and continuing with pathetic and futile pieties that drove Joseph Conrad, quoted now, to remark with sarcasm that it would have been "finer if the band of the Titanic had been quietly saved, instead of being drowned while playing," and then posthumously (and improperly) honored as heroes. The last paragraph, whose cadences could easily enough accommodate a metrical presentation, continues the poet's meditation, which gradually rises to passionate apostrophe in a series of rhetorical questions. In these is exposed the vulnerability of all human life, which no culture, not just that of the *belle époque,* can protect:

> When he was breaking bread and drinking wine.
> They were being born, they desired, they died,
> My God, what crowds! How is it possible
> That all of them wanted to live and are no more?
>
> A teacher leads a flock of five-year-olds
> Through the marble halls of a museum.
> She seats them on the floor, polite boys
> And girls, facing a huge painting,
> And explains: "A helmet, a sword, the gods,
> A mountain, white clouds, an eagle, lightning."
> She is knowing, they see for the first time.
> Her fragile throat, her female organs,

Her multicolored dress, creams, and trinkets
Are embraced by forgiveness. What is not embraced
By forgiveness? Lack of knowledge, innocent unconcern
Would cry for vengeance, demand a verdict
Had I been a judge. I won't be, I'm not.
In splendor the earth's poor moment renews itself.
Simultaneously, now, here, every day
Bread is changed into flesh, wine into blood,
And the impossible, what no one can bear,
Is again accepted and acknowledged.

I'm consoling you, of course. Consoling myself also.
Not very much consoled. Trees-candelabra
And has there ever been anything that offered protection?
Fatality, nameless and pitiless, could it be averted? O civilized
   humanity! O spells, O amulets.

And we have come full circle to Ela's revelation, "it is not like that at all." But her revelation was only partial—the ecstasy. Here we also have the pessimism, added and added until the pessimism all but overwhelms the ecstasy. For what inspires ecstasy—the vividly actual, the richly sensuous, the experiences of the unique individual—seem as nothing against the huge, impersonal powers of history and nature. Individuals, wandering the far reaches of the world, Milosz's father, Ela, Valuev, Peterson, and even the "bony Nansen," are breathtakingly fragile against catastrophe, natural or human. No political system, no transport, however economical, and no cultural amulet will save them. In this Milosz comes closer to Greek tragedy than perhaps anywhere else in his work. We leave the poem with a sense that pathos permeates all our experience, that we are destined for ruin and take our brief joys in the blind moments between the vast grindings of impersonal cause and effect. A harsh conclusion.

But "La Belle Epoque" is not the conclusion to "New Poems" or to *Collected Poems*. That pride of place belongs to the last poem in the series, "Six Lectures in Verse." Here all the strands are gathered, and there is a delicate balance between ecstasy and pessimism:

Boundless history lasted in that moment
Carry their green candles. And magnolias bloom.
This too is real. The din ceases.
Memory closes down its dark waters.
And those, as if behind a glass, stare out, silent.   (492–493)

If we are not entirely consoled by this, we are reminded that reality is greater and at times, as in Greek tragedy, more splendid than any concept we have of it. It is bound to mock whatever pose we strike before its mystery, until we too, as if behind glass, stare out, silent.

Bibliography and
Abbreviations

BW   *Bells in Winter,* trans. Czeslaw Milosz and Lillian Vallee. New York: Ecco Press, 1978.

CCM   Ewa Czarnecka and Aleksander Fiut, *Conversations with Czeslaw Milosz,* trans. Richard Lourie. New York: Harcourt, Brace, 1987.

CM   *The Captive Mind,* trans. Jane Zielonko. New York: Knopf, 1953.

CP   *The Collected Poems, 1931–1987.* New York: Ecco Press, 1988; Viking Penguin, 1988.

EE   *Emperor of the Earth: Modes of Eccentric Vision.* Berkeley: University of California Press, 1977.

HPL   *The History of Polish Literature.* New York: Macmillan, 1969. Rev. ed., Berkeley: University of California Press, 1983.

IS   *The Invincible Song: A Clandestine Anthology* (reprint ed., *Piesn niepodlegla*). Ann Arbor: Michigan Slavic Publications, 1981.

IV   *The Issa Valley,* trans. Louis Iribarne. New York: Farrar, Straus and Giroux, 1981.

LU   *The Land of Ulro,* trans. Louis Iribarne. New York: Farrar, Straus and Giroux, 1984.

NL   *Nobel Lecture.* New York: Farrar, Straus and Giroux, 1981.

NR   *Native Realm: A Search for Self-Definition,* trans. Catherine S. Leach. Garden City: Doubleday, 1968.

PPP   *Postwar Polish Poetry: An Anthology,* ed. Czeslaw Milosz. Garden City: Doubleday, 1965. Rev. ed., Berkeley: University of California Press, 1983.

SN   *The Separate Notebooks,* trans. Robert Hass and Robert Pinsky, with the author and Renata Gorczynski. New York: Ecco Press, 1984.

SP   *Selected Poems,* trans. "several hands," intro. Kenneth Rexroth. New York: Seabury Press, 1973; Ecco Press, 1980.

TSP   *The Seizure of Power,* trans. Celina Wieniewska. New York: Criterion Books, 1955; Farrar, Straus and Giroux, 1982.

UE   *Unattainable Earth,* trans. Czeslaw Milosz and Robert Hass. New York: Ecco Press, 1986.

VSF   *Visions from San Francisco Bay,* trans. Richard Lourie. New York: Farrar, Straus and Giroux, 1982.

WP   *The Witness of Poetry.* Cambridge: Harvard University Press, 1983.

Notes

1. San Francisco Bay

1. Lewis Hyde, "The Devil and Mr. Milosz," *Nation,* September 22, 1989, p. 278. A notable exception to our generalization about reviews of *Visions* was Scott Mahler's "A New Introduction to Milosz," *In Print* 11 (1982), 4.

2. Poland

1. Thus we cannot agree with Judith Dompkowski's characterization of the poetry of this period: "Milosz tried to move beyond himself and join the natural world he thought to be benevolent. By allying himself with a powerful force, he sought to prevent his own annihilation in face of the coming disasters." *Down a Spiral Staircase, Never-Ending* (New York: Peter Lang, 1990), p. 83. Nature is not seen as benevolent and cannot preserve the poet from annihilation.

2. The reader particularly interested in this poem should consult the interpretation offered by Jan Blonski in his "Poetry and Knowledge," *World Literature Today* 52 (1978), 387–391; this special Milosz issue, edited by Ivan Ivask, is hereafter abbreviated *WLT.* Blonski regards the poem as an inten-

tionally "unresolved contention over the source and destiny of poetry." As much as we admire the careful attention Blonski has given the poem, we do not find his conclusion convincing; perhaps we should add that Milosz apparently doesn't either (see CCM, 114).

3. Milosz has not included this poem in any of his English translations. We are using the version made by Madeline Levine in her *Contemporary Polish Poetry, 1925–1975* (Boston: G. K. Hall, 1981), pp. 38–39. But see "Father Ch., Many Years Later" (CP, 425). Still worth reading, by the way, is the first attempt in English to sketch Milosz's early development as a poet: Zbigniew Foleyewski, "Czeslaw Milosz: A Poet's Road to Ithaca Between Worlds, Wars, and Poetics," *Books Abroad* 43 (1969), 17–24.

4. Stanislaw Baranczak, "A Black Mirror at the End of the Tunnel," *Polish Review* 31 (1986), 276–284. This essay on "Dawns" is probably the best treatment available in English of any early poem of Milosz.

5. This seems to be Aleksander Fuit's view when he writes of the conclusion: "No one is without blame; everyone is both victim and executioner." *Eternal Moment: The Poetry of Czeslaw Milosz* (Berkeley: University of California Press, 1990), p. 46.

6. We are quoting here from the version by Robert Hass and Robert Pinsky in SN, 130–151. This translation tries to replicate the original rhyme pattern, at the expense of literal sense. Milosz's own translation in CP is more literal. On the problems presented by this cycle, see Robert Hass, "'The World': A Note on Translation," *Ironwood* 18 (1981); 37–40. Lillian Vallee in the same issue discusses the problems of interpretation in "What is *The World*? (A Naive Essay)," pp. 130–139.

7. See Donald Davie, "Milosz' War-Time Poems," appendix to *Czeslaw Milosz and the Insufficiency of Lyric* (Knoxville: University of Tennessee Press, 1986). We owe much to Davie's view of the unity of the cycle but disagree with him on a number of specifics, especially about its concluding poems.

8. Quoted in Bogdana Carpenter, *The Poetic Avant Garde in Poland, 1918–1939* (Seattle: University of Washington Press, 1983), p. 196. "Capitalist bedbugs" is an allusion to Vladimir Mayakovsky's play *The Bedbug*. Mayakovsky, for Milosz the most important Slavic writer to see art in political terms, had turned his considerable literary talents to Bolshevik propaganda. This allusion had its own bite, for Mayakovsky killed himself just the year before. Milosz later wrote, "For me the Russian Revolution was personified not by Lenin but by Vladimir Mayakovsky" (NR, 123).

9. Milosz, it must be emphasized, was prepared to do literary work of a purely political character. His other major publishing venture with the

Resistance was a translation into Polish of *Au travers le désastre* by Jacques Maritain, the prominent philosopher who was a spokesman for the Free French. Milosz translated this work, as he made clear in his preface, to counteract "totalitarian propaganda" that the "fall of France heralded the fall of democracy all over the world" (1S, viii). The reference to totalitarian propaganda, however, could apply as easily to the Marxists as to the Nazis.

10. Milosz himself published an essay on Witkiewicz in 1943, perhaps the first to be written after that poet's death.

3. Paris

1. See Paul Coates, "Irony and Choice: Milosz in the Late Forties and Early Fifties," in Edward Mozejko, ed., *Between Anxiety and Hope: The Poetry and Writings of Czeslaw Milosz* (Edmonton: University of Alberta Press, 1988), pp. 134–140. This contains translations of passages from "The Plain" as well as a provocative contrast between Milosz and Witold Gombrowicz, the leading Polish novelist of this period.

2. Of the many reviews of CM that appeared at the time of its original publication, the best one remains Dwight MacDonald's in *The New Yorker*, November 7, 1953, pp. 173–182.

3. *The Simone Weil Reader*, ed. George A. Panichas (New York: David McKay, 1977), p. 417.

4. Coates, "Irony and Choice," p. 140. The best treatment of Milosz's gallery of captive minds is found in Madeline Levine's "Warnings to the West: Czeslaw Milosz's Political Prose of the 1950's," *Between Anxiety and Hope*, pp. 112–133. As Levine points out, the portraits are easily enough identified by anyone familiar with the Polish literary scene of the time.

5. After the publication of CM, Milosz received an admiring letter from the American Trappist monk, Thomas Merton, who had recently become famous for his own autobiography. This began a correspondence that ended only with Merton's death. In his earliest letters Milosz refers to himself as a "lapsed catastrophist," urges Merton to read Simone Weil (as evidence he cites Camus's opinion that she is the purest spirit of the twentieth century), and criticizes his own book because, in anger at those intellectuals who had chosen to stay captive in falsehood or error, he had not conveyed the love he still felt for them.

6. Milosz was not unfamiliar with such heresies. During his reading as a schoolboy he became a "secret taster of Manichean poisons" (CP, 303)—but the fascination then was the intense drama of a gnostic mythology.

7. An exception to this is, not surprisingly, Milosz's translator Lillian Vallee in her "*The Valley of Issa:* An Interpretation," *WLT,* pp. 403–407. Nonetheless, even Milosz's perceptive interviewer Ewa Czarneck has trouble on this point; see CCM, 166–167.

8. Milosz, "Speaking of a Mammal," *Confluence* 5 (1957), 26. This journal was edited by a young Harvard professor, Henry Kissinger.

9. Milosz, "A Notebook: Born by Lake Leman," available in English as the epigraph to Aleksander Fiut's *Eternal Moment.*

10. Lest the importance of the *Treatise* seem primarily personal, we should cite Edward Mozejko's judgment: "In the annals of twentieth-century Polish literature, this is the most ambitious and significant poetic work" (*Between Anxiety and Hope,* p. 25).

11. As usual, however, Milosz follows this affirmation with a qualification: "Yet since this entire image is in the conditional and has to serve as a proof of the insufficiency of words, it is not a description that would satisfy the poet and is at best an outline, a project" (WP, 73).

12. As Alexander Coleman puts it in his essay on NR: "It is within: that is where the native realm lies." "The Still Point in Milosz' *Native Realm,*" *WLT,* pp. 399–403.

4. A Magic Mountain

1. For an intelligent reading of *Visions* that emphasizes the distance from Europe but misses the importance of Dostoevsky, see Olga Sherer, "To Ulro through San Francisco Bay," *WLT,* pp. 408–412.

2. For Miller's version of their early encounters, see his *Big Sur and the Oranges of Hieronymous Bosch* (New York: New Directions, 1964), pp. 218–220.

3. This purpose is implied by an eventual change of title. In *Selected Poems* it is "*The* Task"; in *Collected Poems* it is "*A* Task."

4. In its setting as part of *King Popiel* a poem like "No More" can be read as an ironic retreat from hopeless engagement with reality, but in *Selected Poems* it can be taken as an acceptance of moderation.

5. Oscar's first impression of his young relative deserves to be recorded: "I had the pleasure this summer of making the acquaintance of my nephew . . . I expected a horror to appear, a monster worthy of the rest of my family . . . How surprised I was to find myself before a physically attractive young man of 19, a poet at once most zealous and well-balanced, moved with feelings of respect for my work, very attached to the intelligent and

venerable side of monarchist, Catholic, and aristocratic tradition, and a little Communist—just what is needed to do useful work in our unbelievable epoch—in a word, a young gentleman whom I consider a little as my son." Oscar Milosz, *The Noble Traveller,* ed. Christopher Bamford (West Stockbridge, Mass.: Lindisfarne Press, 1985), p. 472.

6. Milosz later discovered the writings of Swedenborg and regarded them as an independent corroboration of his vision. Czeslaw remembers finding written in the margin of Oscar's copy of Swedenborg: "In the name of the Father, Son, and Holy Spirit, this is what I saw."

7. This true understanding of Oscar Milosz took place gradually, over a long period of time. Even the few pages given to Oscar in *Native Realm* emphasize the difference between Czeslaw's original and later estimates of his elder. He admitted that Oscar's works originally "aroused mixed feelings, sometimes even strong hostility." He explains, "My intelligence remained disturbingly disproportionate to my development" (172–173).

5. The World, Again

1. See Jan Blonski, "Poetry and Knowledge," *WLT,* p. 388.

2. Mikhail Bakhtin, *Problems of Dostoevsky's Poetics,* trans. Caryl Emerson (Minneapolis: University of Minnesota Press, 1984), p. 3.

3. We ought to register a proviso here concerning just how free, how unconditioned by authorial intent, are the characters of polyphonic art. Poetry is, even in its most relaxed forms, highly selective discourse, and a highly patterned one. This suggests that the free-for-all or pandemonium of radical polyphony is not an option it can draw on without qualification. It seems to us that the term, a metaphor in any case when applied to the linguistic arts, must be used in relation to both Dostoevsky and Milosz in the following sense: discourse in which a selected number of representative voices are put into conflicting relation, on the condition that the author allows these voices credibility. The voices taken together would then constitute the whole range of serious response to an issue and give readers a sense of plenitude, as if no serious voice has been excluded, no opposition unheard, although the poem must serve as a synecdoche for an ideal or imagined plenitude of treatment. So in this way we agree with Fiut's conclusion: "The concept of polyphony can be accurately applied to Milosz' poetry but remains inadequate" (*Eternal Moment,* p. 155).

4. Stanislaw Baranczak, "Milosz' Poetic Language," *Language and Style* 18 (1985), 319–333.

5. Milosz, when asked about this, chose not to answer directly, giving instead a description of the poem's piecemeal composition, which in the spirit of "Ars Poetica?" leaves the question still begging. See CCM, 237ff.

6. Tomas Venclova, "Czeslaw Milosz' Despair and Grace," *WLT,* p. 394.

7. Milosz's deeply moving poem "On Parting with My Wife, Janina" (CP, 459–460) concludes with an evocation of this resurrection of the flesh.

8. The issue of *apokatastasis* is complex. It seems to appear first as a secular technical term, referring to the return of the sun or moon after an eclipse. As a theological concept, it would be opposed by the church if interpreted as excluding eternal punishment. But orthodox thinkers preserved the concept when they could avoid its exotic implications, such as the salvation of devils. One strand of gnosticism looked toward the restoration of an original perfection. Milosz's own hesitation when questioned about the term suggests its burden of complexity (see CCM, 247–248).

9. The title in the Polish original was "From the Rising of the Sun to Its Setting."

10. Key points in Socinian doctrine were the denial of Christ's divinity and rationalist explanations of sin and salvation.

11. Milosz reveals an amazing continuity in his poetry and thought. Here are lines from "Bells in Winter" explaining time and the end of time:

For me, therefore, everything has a double existence.
Both in time and when time shall be no more.   (CP, 310)

And from "A Book in the Ruins" (1941):

Only when two times, two forms are drawn
Together and their legibility
Disturbed, do I see that immortality
Is not very different from the present
And is for its sake.   (CP, 29)

12. Compare this with Milosz's treatment in HPL, 411–412, where he says that Czechowicz "can be included in the 'catastrophist' trend."

13. This is also true of the Polish version, published in *Hymn of the Pearl* (1981), though the poems in the two volumes are not identical; for example, "Ode to a Bird" was published in the (Polish) *King Popiel and Other Poems* (1962). Nor are the poems appearing in the Polish and English volumes presented in the same order. "Reading the Japanese Poet Issa (1762–1826)"

precedes "The Separate Notebooks" in *Hymn of the Pearl* but comes after it in SN.

14. "Solidarity," of course, is also an allusion to the Polish workers' movement. When a monument was unveiled in Gdansk to those who died there, it bore lines from Milosz's poem "You Who Have Wronged."

6. Milosz Collected

1. This reordering is not without its anomalies. For example, between *Bobo's Metamorphosis* (1965) and *From the Rising of the Sun* (1974) we find a cluster of five called "Uncollected Poems." In fact, *Collected Poems* is itself no simple mirror of Milosz's poetic career, for it is also "selected," since not all the Polish originals have been translated, especially those from the earliest period. There is no doubt that adding, subtracting, and rearranging will make some difference to a reading of Milosz the poet. A detailed study of *Collected* and the earlier books in English would doubtless show subtle shifts of emphasis, a slightly different local field of nuance. But the whole is left intact: the large decisive patterns are still there and, if anything, are reinforced. If *Collected* has superseded all the earlier books (and this is arguable), it has done so at no cost to the kinds of experiences we have come to expect from this poet. From the *Selected Poems* on, there is a certain shape not just in individual poems but in the books themselves.

2. This is the "beautiful cousin Ela" of "The Wormwood Star" (CP, 374).

3. One of the most moving of the new poems, "In a Jar" (CP, 448), is about newts.

4. Taken from Wyn Craig Wade, *The Titanic: End of a Dream* (New York: Rawson, Wade, 1979). The *Titanic*, the reader may remember, is associated with cousin Ela (and Schopenhauer) in *The Separate Notebooks*. See the passage quoted on p. 125 above.

Acknowledgments

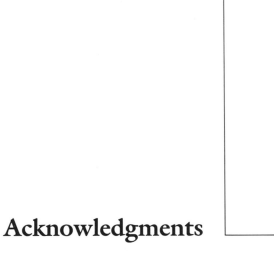

The authors wish to thank those who helped—above all, Thomas D'Evelyn and Joyce Backman of Harvard University Press; also Sherry Irving, Maggie Rebhan, Laurie Saunders, Carol Nash, Barney Roddy, Kirsten Anderson, and Rebecca Kidd. To the subject of this book many thanks for his patience, encouragement, and broad smiles of affirmation. Finally, we bow to each other for making two very different styles work together in a higher cause. But what, as they say, are friends for?

Index

Library of Congress Cataloging-in-Publication Data

Nathan, Leonard, 1924–
    The poet's work: an introduction to Czeslaw Milosz / Leonard Nathan and Arthur
Quinn.
       p. cm.
    Includes bibliographical references and index.
    ISBN 0-674-68969-0 (cloth)   ISBN 0-674-68970-4 (paper)
       1. Milosz, Czeslaw (1911–   )—Criticism and interpretation. I. Quinn, Arthur. II. Title.
PG7158.M5532N38 1991   91-4443
891.8'58709—dc20   CIP